Transforming Primary Care

Personal medical services in the new NHS

Edited by Richard Lewis and Stephen Gillam

Published by
King's Fund Publishing
11–13 Cavendish Square
London W1M 0AN

© King's Fund 1999

First published 1999
Reprinted 2000

ISBN 1 85717 290 6

A CIP catalogue record for this book is available from the British Library

Available from:

King's Fund Bookshop
11–13 Cavendish Square
London
W1M 0AN

Tel: 0207 307 2591
Fax: 0207 307 2801

Printed and bound in Great Britain

Typeset by Peter Powell Origination & Print Limited

Contents

Acknowledgements

We would like to thank our colleagues at the NPCRDC in Manchester and, of course, the nine first wave pilots that form the basis of this project.

We are also very grateful to Angela Coulter, John Eversley and Martin Roland for their comments on work in progress.

Foreword

Over the decades successive Secretaries of State for Health have suffered from a shared delusion, overriding differences of party and ideology. This is that central government can change the way in which health care is delivered by changing the NHS's organisational structure. In the outcome, it has become apparent that while structural change may facilitate or impede change, the NHS's dynamics largely reflect other factors: evolving professional and public attitudes, developments in the technology of health care, demographic and other social pressures. While politicians flatter themselves that they are driving change, producing and directing the play, in fact the script is being written by others. The real revolutions in the NHS, it is tempting to argue, stem less from top-down initiatives than from bottom-up innovations and experiments.

This book represents an illuminating and highly significant case study of this process at work. It reports on the Personal Medical Services pilots. These are the experiments made possible but not mandated – the difference is crucial – by the NHS (Primary Care) Act 1997. The Act allows practices, trusts and other NHS bodies to employ general practitioners on a salaried basis. Further, it allows such schemes to be nurse-led, with salaried GPs in a supporting role. Some 80 pilot schemes are now operating. Another wave has just been launched. The schemes are concentrated in inner city and other deprived areas where it has traditionally been most difficult to attract general practitioners.

As the various chapters in the book show, the schemes vary considerably in character. They will, no doubt, also vary considerably in their effectiveness and durability. But this, in a sense, is precisely the strength of the permissive approach of the 1997 Act, as distinct from the prescriptive strategy that has been the NHS norm. It allows local innovations in response to local circumstances, permitting the purchasers of health care to take the initiative in developing primary health care to match needs. It inaugurates a process of institutional natural selection that may over the next few decades transform the delivery of primary care in the UK.

This is a large claim to make. But in the perspective of the NHS's history, the PMS pilots signal a radical change of direction. In 1948, and subsequently, the medical profession had one consistent and dominating aim: to maintain the status of GPs as independent contractors. It was the spectre of a salaried service that prompted a frenzy of opposition to Bevan's legislation setting up the NHS. The fact that the profession has now accepted the notion of salaried GPs – even of GPs employed by nurses, a notion which would have produced mass apoplexy 50 or even 20 years ago – suggests that professional attitudes have been transformed, so making possible a whole range of new permutations in the organisation and delivery of primary care.

This transformation is both explained and reinforced by a variety of underlying professional and social trends. The younger generation of doctors – and, in particular, the women among them who will soon represent a majority of the profession, as they already represent a majority of graduates – no longer subscribes unreservedly to the idea that professionalism demands an open ended and unlimited commitment of time. The relationship between the medical and nursing profession is being renegotiated; increasingly, as with NHS Direct, it is nurses who seem to be replacing GPs as the gatekeepers to the NHS (although it remains to be seen how acceptable or effective this turns out to be).

So this book is a report on what may turn out to be the beginning of a quiet, incremental revolution in primary health care, whose reverberations will be felt throughout the whole system. Whether the example of the PMS pilots will also serve as a model for the policy making process in the NHS – by persuading governments that they can best promote change by enabling innovation and experiment rather than by issuing directives and blueprints – is another matter.

Rudolf Klein

Contributors

Ian Ayres	Chief Executive, Nelson Primary Care Group
Tom Butler	Chief Executive, Chester City Primary Care Group
Tim Crossley	General Practitioner
Stephen Gillam	Director, Primary Care Programme, King's Fund
Toby Gosden	Research Associate in Health Economics, National Primary Care Research and Development Centre
Alison Holbourn	Primary Care Project Manager, North Cheshire Health Authority and Warrington Community Health Care Trust, and Honorary Research Fellow, National Primary Care Research and Development Centre
Clare Jenkins	Project Officer, Personal Medical Services, King's Fund
Diane Jones	Fellow in Development and Dissemination, National Primary Care Research and Development Centre
Richard Lewis	Visiting Fellow, King's Fund
Nicholas Mays	Health Adviser, Social Policy Branch, The Treasury, Wellington, New Zealand and Visiting Professor, Department of Public Health and Policy, London School of Hygiene and Tropical Medicine and Department of Social Policy and Administration, London School of Economics and Political Science
Rod Sheaff	Senior Research Fellow, National Primary Care Research and Development Centre

Chapter 1

Introduction

Richard Lewis and Stephen Gillam

The NHS has frequently been subject to root and branch reform, with the periodic importation of new forms, cultures and languages. By contrast, primary care (and more specifically general medical practice) has retained many of its key characteristics since 1948. During the last decade, however, pressure for change has increased – from government, management and the medical profession itself. They suggested that the consensus over the status quo was under pressure and that major change was imminent.

In 1997 the NHS (Primary Care) Act was to be the catalyst for change. The legislation completed its passage through Parliament as one of the last actions of the outgoing Major Government and survived the change of government relatively intact. The Act enabled the piloting of new forms of primary medical services, known originally as Primary Care Act Pilot Schemes (PCAPS) but later renamed Personal Medical Services (PMS) pilots. A modest first wave of pilots went live from April 1998. The second wave, to go live in October 1999, is significantly larger.

Since the Act was passed, of course, the British health service has been plunged into further reform, being reinvented under the Blair Government as 'the new NHS'. Primary care has been at the heart of this revolution, with primary care groups (PCGs) taking centre stage. The relationship between PCGs and PMS pilots has, at times, been tense – with both initiatives competing for limited development time and resources – and the strategic linkage between the two has not always been clear. However, PMS pilots are beginning to provide PCGs with a new tool for the development of primary care services and may offer new models of good practice that can be transferred more widely (within a local area or beyond).

The material upon which this book is based has been drawn from a development project run jointly by the King's Fund and the National Primary Care Research and Development Centre (NPCRDC) at Manchester University. A network of nine first wave PMS pilot sites has been established for the purposes of service development and evaluation, with a clear mandate to share early learning as quickly and as widely as possible. This book is based on the experiences of the sites during their six-month preparation phase and first year of operation.

This book has three main concerns:

1. to describe the policy context within which these pilots have developed
2. to present the evidence and learning to date in relation to the implementation of the pilots
3. to consider the implications of PMS pilots for the future.

Chapters 2, 3 and 4 set the scene. First, Lewis and Mays explore the roots of the PMS initiative through an analysis of primary care policy over the last ten years. Paradoxically, it is continuities in the development of health policy – despite the change of government – that most impress these authors. In Chapter 3 Jenkins gives a detailed account of PMS and the nature of the first wave of pilots. The description of first and second wave sites in Chapter 4 illustrates the heterogeneity of the pilot schemes and suggests that many will be meeting priority health needs.

Key themes identified in these opening chapters are examined in greater detail in subsequent chapters. 'Nurse-led' primary care attracts increasing attention as a possible solution to problems of access and medical recruitment in urban areas. As Chapter 5 shows, lead nurses at many of the first wave sites are justifiably enthusiastic about their achievements, but Jones also looks at problems they face in developing their services. General practitioners remain sharply divided over the arguments for and against salaried practice. Gosden and colleagues are in no doubt that these opportunities are likely to expand. Chapter 6 therefore looks at the practicalities of establishing salaried posts. Behind the outward manifestations of PMS lies a process of local contracting. Crucial questions are still to be answered regarding the potential gains of moving from a uniform national contract to local arrangements supposedly more sensitive to local needs. In Chapter 7, Sheaff provides fascinating insights from painstaking analysis of the first round of contracts. While these expose the limitations of current 'paper and process', he remains cautiously optimistic for future waves. Chapter 8 considers information management and the experience of first wave sites in developing appropriate IT systems.

Learning from these core chapters is pulled together in the conclusion. The book is consistently analytical in tone, with data presented where available. It is structured to be read sequentially but the contributions stand alone. All contributors have been directly involved in supporting the first wave of PMS sites through working on the NPCRDC/King's Fund collaboration mentioned above. An appendix provides details of the nine sites involved; they are the source for many of the examples and case studies used in the text. Indeed, Chapter 9 provides a vision of what two of these projects are starting to put into place. They graphically illustrate what opportunities PMS and the establishment of primary care trusts provide for the transformation of primary and community care.

Chapter 2

Trends in Government health policy – from GMS to PMS

Richard Lewis and Nicholas Mays

KEY POINTS

- General medical services have been structurally stable since the inception of the NHS

- During the 1990s the national GP contract has provided a tool to increase the accountability of GPs, to direct clinical activity towards specific services and to introduce cash limits

- The national GP contract failed to address some deep rooted deficits in primary care and was criticised for its lack of local flexibility

- *Choice and Opportunity* and the NHS (Primary Care) Act 1997 provided the opportunity for local contracting for primary care together with the introduction of new providers and salaried GPs

- PMS pilots have been incorporated into 'the new NHS', the Labour Government's replacement for the 'internal market'

- Successive governments have used incremental change when dealing with general medical services and the final destination of policy is still not clear

---

Health policy since the 1980s – a brief review

General medical services (GMS – the family doctor service provided by GPs and their teams) have proved structurally perhaps the most stable element of the NHS. While the hospital and community health services (HCHS) have undergone radical transformations, such as the introduction of general management under the Griffiths reforms[1] and the internal market under the 1990 NHS reforms,[2] the key structural characteristics of GMS have remained largely unchanged since the inception of the NHS in 1948.

There are three key pillars upon which the organisation of GMS has rested throughout most of the history of the NHS: services are GP-led (i.e. other staff within the primary health care team have generally been subordinate to GPs); those GPs form small businesses independently contracted to the NHS; and GPs' terms and conditions are negotiated nationally, ensuring a degree of consistency (in the contract specification, if not in service delivery) nationwide. The sometimes-bitter disputes between government and the profession over the content of the contract notwithstanding, general practice has retained a significant level of professional autonomy and clear separation from the hospital service through a national contract. Elsewhere in the NHS, the last 15 years have seen turbulence and the radical reshaping of the local organisational forms and values that form the National Health Service.

The NHS policy agenda has been dominated by a number of problems, not least concerns about the efficiency of the service (as health spending rose inexorably during the 1980s), variations in quality and accessibility, and the relative lack of obligations on professionals to consider the cost of treatment in their management of patients. A number of strategies emerged to strengthen management, involve clinicians in budgetary management and encourage competition.[3, 4, 5]

The Griffiths reforms of 1983 introduced a general management hierarchy to 'performance manage' the HCHS part of the NHS, together with new and tighter lines of accountability between health authorities and the centre. Commercial practices were introduced through the often controversial 'contracting out' of ancillary services via competitive tendering. Of perhaps more long-term significance, however, was the attempt to bind hospital clinicians more closely to the processes of management and budgeting through the Resource Management Initiative, piloted in six hospitals from 1986.[6] Primary care, particularly general practice, remained outside the scope of these changes.

The creation of the internal market in the early 1990s drew GPs (largely in their role as care 'purchasers') into new relationships with the 'mainstream' of the NHS through the mechanism of GP fundholding. Competition in the internal market was to be generated through the formalisation of 'principal–agent' relationships (known more colloquially as the purchaser/provider split) and the creation of quasi-independent NHS trusts separate from health authorities, which were to act as health care purchasers. This mechanism was designed to encourage corporate competition for resources on the part of providers which would, in theory at least, foster cost-conscious behaviour. It also served to draw hospital clinicians into management as a necessary means of securing their clinical activity and relating this activity to the terms of the new contracts agreed between NHS trusts and health authorities.

GP fundholding provided an even more direct example of clinician-centred budget holding, since it allowed individual practices the opportunity to reap the rewards of effective financial management in the form of retained 'savings'. However, the evidence for the effectiveness of the internal market and GP fundholding, against the policy criteria of the Government, is mixed.[7] GP fundholding, for example, was associated with a lower rise in the costs of prescribing and lower waiting times for specialist care, but appeared to make no difference to overall rates of referral or to the level of patient choice.[8]

It is ironic that the general practice as 'provider' of services should have been left relatively untouched by the sweeping reforms of the 'internal market', since GP fundholding was introduced primarily as a *purchasing* innovation (although fundholding budgets also incorporated GP prescribing costs). After all, a contract had, at least formally, underpinned relations between government and the GPs since 1948. However, the internal market model introduced in 1991 did not include local contracting for the services of GPs and their staff. Nevertheless, there were significant changes: indicative drug budgets were introduced for GPs, with real drug budgets for volunteer GP fundholders; prescribing advisers were introduced; and weak family practitioner committees were replaced by the managerially-stronger family health services authorities (FHSAs). Resources used to support and develop general practice and its infrastructure were cash-limited, with discretion over their expenditure given to the new FHSAs.

Radical policy developments (i.e. those introducing systemic change) in the last decade, in so far as they have focused on primary care, have primarily concentrated on the role of the GP as 'purchaser' and 'gatekeeper' to specialist services,[9] with a secondary concern being the GP as prescriber. However, despite the stable structural framework and an incremental approach to policy development, primary care itself has not been wholly sheltered from change. As with the HCHS sector, the twin objectives of budgetary control and clinical accountability have influenced policy development (for more detail on policy development in general medical services, see Glendinning, 1999[10]).

Expenditure within primary care had risen quickly during the 1980s, indeed faster than that on HCHS.[11] Spending on GP prescribing was demand-led with no budgetary cap and this, consequently, hindered the Government's ability to control overall health spending.[12] At the same time, GPs had hitherto been considered 'unaccountable', in that their terms of service were largely unspecified and consisted of customary practice as defined by GPs themselves. Increasingly, government wished to measure the performance of GPs and to hold them accountable for specific activities, in return for payment. Allied to this was a desire to direct clinical behaviour towards activities felt to be 'worth-while' and therefore to reduce the autonomy of GPs in determining what they would do and to whom. Finally, there was a long-standing interest (particularly from the Treasury) in finding a way of cash-limiting the demand-driven parts of GMS, including the costs of GPs' prescribing.

The 1990 contract, which was 'imposed' on general practice in the face of fierce opposition by a bullish Government, represented a new government/professional relationship.[13, 14] However, while the contract itself represented 'top-down' policy-making, the new policy aims were to be achieved through explicit financial incentives rather than through managerial compulsion.

The new contract introduced target payments for particular clinical activities (such as screening and immunisation), thus using financial rewards to deliver desired public health outcomes. It also significantly increased the proportion of GP remuneration obtained through capitation payments, in an attempt to generate greater competition for patients among practitioners as well as to encourage GPs to focus on health promotion. The 1990 contract represented an attempt to introduce a clearer 'principal–agent' relationship to primary care by breathing life into a hitherto moribund contract.

As the financial incentives incorporated into the new contract began to bite, concerns were expressed over the result. In particular, the arrangements for paying GPs to undertake health promotion activities had led to a steep rise in the number of GP clinics of dubious efficacy. In addition, the distribution of resources for the clinics (e.g. well women clinics) did not appear to be related to need.[15] In 1992, the GP contract was amended so that GPs were no longer paid simply to hold health promotion clinics, but had to achieve results and collect data on what they had done.

The national structure of the new contract was also, by its very nature, rigid and did not reflect the different needs of local populations – except to take account of differences in their age structure. Enhanced capitation payments were made in relation to patients with social and demographic characteristics associated with higher GP workload (the so-called 'Jarman score'). However, this innovation was criticised for relative insensitivity. Practices, particularly in the inner city, continued to complain that deprivation and high patient mobility prevented them from achieving the target payments introduced by the new contract, thus leaving them financially disadvantaged. The approach continued to be one of developing *national* solutions to local problems.

The national basis of the contract also limited the aspirations of the new FHSAs. They were created to provide management and leadership in primary care, but found their power to assure quality and develop new forms of primary medical service constrained. GPs were accountable for performance against a contract negotiated directly between the Government and the General Medical Services Committee (GMSC, later the General Practice Committee) of the British Medical Association (BMA). This shielded them from attempts by local FHSA management to vary and interpret their terms of service just as they had been protected from the former FPCs. This was frustrating for FHSAs, not least because they were aware that significant variations in quality existed in primary care, which they believed could be alleviated by locally sensitive forms of contract and incentives. This issue was particularly visible in London, where a deficit in primary care in the capital had long been identified.[16, 17] Despite the injection of significant developmental resources, the 'gap' between London and the rest of England in terms of the range of services available and the physical infrastructure of primary care stubbornly persisted.[18, 19]

During the 1990s, FHSAs developed new approaches to developing quality in general practice.[20] However, these were, by their very nature, voluntary and proved difficult to enforce. When deficiencies in services were identified, it was by no means certain that GPs would agree to take part in local quality schemes. Difficulties were also experienced in recruiting GPs, particularly in the inner city. FHSAs went to increasingly elaborate lengths to find new GPs, sometimes recruiting as far away as Australia. A range of unofficial schemes to encourage salaried practice emerged in a few places,[21] and the London Initiative Zone introduced new, but temporary, flexibilities that assisted with the recruitment of additional doctors.

The 1990s also saw a change to the organisational structure of local health agencies. The early 1990s saw FHSAs and district health authorities begin to integrate, often achieving *de facto* mergers through the creation of 'health commissions'. In April 1996 new health authorities were formally created and there ceased to be a separate organisational focus for primary care contractor services.

Breaking the mould? *Choice and Opportunity*

The publication in 1996 of two White Papers (*Primary Care the Future – Choice and Opportunity* and *Primary Care – Delivering the Future*) and the NHS (Primary Care) Act 1997 that followed, marked the beginning of the end for this period of gradual reform of primary care and, perhaps, the end of the automatic majority against reform among GPs. While the Government described its approach as 'essentially evolutionary', it set in train forces that have the potential to revolutionise the fundamental characteristics of NHS primary care. These forces are discussed in detail in subsequent chapters.

Choice and Opportunity emerged out of a six-month 'listening exercise' undertaken by the Minister for Health, Gerald Malone, and built on initiatives that were already underway.[22] It was as much a response to pressure for change from within primary care as a 'top-down' policy initiative. The Secretary of State for Health was quick to point this out.[23] The GMSC of the BMA had, in the early 1990s, begun to re-evaluate some of the key aspects of the work and organisation of general practice. In particular, the compulsory contractual requirement to provide 24-hour responsibility for care was the subject of extensive negotiations. The apparently ever-expanding expectations placed on the modern GP had led to a desire within the profession to define strictly the meaning of 'core' general medical services.[24, 25] At the same time, the BMA had also become alarmed about recruitment and retention of doctors, and suggested that general practice was in the throes of a 'deepening workforce crisis'.[26] The 1990 GP contract was seen by all sides as bureaucratic and increasingly problematic, notwithstanding government attempts to streamline its administration,[27] remove those elements most objectionable to the profession and alter those parts which appeared to be encouraging ineffective services (e.g. certain GP health promotion clinics).

It appeared that primary care, and general practice in particular, was ripe for further change. Even the benefits of the long-cherished independent contractor status of GPs were beginning to be challenged from within the profession itself. A survey undertaken on behalf of the GMSC in 1992 had shown that over half of GPs would have liked to become salaried, or would consider salaried status if the right circumstances arose (see Chapter 6).[28]

Primary Care: The Future[29] identified key principles that should underpin the delivery of services and set out a broad agenda that it was hoped would redress the problems that had become associated with primary care (see Box 2.1).

BOX 2.1: *PRIMARY CARE: THE FUTURE* (1996)

Themes emerging from 'the listening exercise':

- resources – equitable distribution, flexible use, appropriate balance between primary and secondary care

- partnership – team work, increasing the non-medical role

- development of professional knowledge – supporting education and research and development

- patient and carer information and involvement

- securing the workforce and premises – GP recruitment, new employment and contracting arrangements, better use of the workforce and improved premises

- better organisation – linking practices, better management and IT, less bureaucracy

- local flexibility – e.g. community trust employed GPs, practice-based contract, extended fundholding

---

The subsequent NHS (Primary Care) Act 1997 delivered new powers to form Primary Care Act pilots (now known as Personal Medical Services pilots). These allowed general medical and dental services to be provided under local contracts and, for the first time, permitted the wide-spread employment of salaried GP principals. A last minute amendment to the legislation also allowed nurse-led pilots (where the prime responsibility for providing primary care services rested with a nurse rather than a GP). The NHS itself was now able to initiate new forms of practice organisation, through the actions of health authorities, rather than simply relying on innovations emerging from within the independent contractor sector.

By the time of its departure in May 1997, the outgoing Conservative Government had prepared the ground for a number of important variations on the traditional model of NHS primary care, albeit largely on a pilot basis. As a result, the following significant changes could be secured:

- the development of an alternative means of employment and service delivery to that of the independent GMS/GDS contractor
- the ending of the monopoly of primary medical care enjoyed by GPs with new market entrants in the shape of NHS trusts and nurses
- the ending of the universal application of the national contract and the 'closed shop' of the GMSC (now GPC)
- the introduction of new models of primary care led by nurses rather than GPs
- the development of new, larger primary care organisations formed through alliances between GP practices and between practices and NHS trusts
- the gradual integration of hitherto separate funding streams of GMS and HCHS.

However, while the pilots were to test important new models of service delivery, they were few in number (see Chapter 3). This breach in the hitherto monolithic national contract had generated opposition within the medical profession[30] and at no stage had the Government suggested that PMS pilots would eventually become compulsory.

New Labour, new policy?

The New NHS White Paper introduced by the Labour Government[31] embraced many of the underlying policy themes of their Conservative predecessors such as improving professional accountability, notwithstanding the attendant rhetoric of reform focused on the abolition of the internal market.

Primary care groups (PCGs) are the centrepiece of Labour's vision for the NHS. PCGs are sub-committees of health authorities formed by local clusters of GPs and primary care nurses charged with improving the health of the community, developing primary and community health services and commissioning secondary services.[32] Over time, PCGs are expected to evolve to become free-standing primary care trusts (PCTs), at the fourth and highest level directly providing services alongside their other responsibilities.

Much about PCGs is redolent of what has gone before.[33] Budget holding principles, developed under GP fundholding and total purchasing pilots (i.e. the extension of standard fundholding to incorporate non-elective services), were extended to all GPs, as were the cash-limited budgets for prescribing operated by fundholders. For the first time, all GPs are subject to a firm drugs budget. Importantly, under 'the new NHS', the purchaser/provider split has been maintained – although contracts have been relabelled 'service agreements'. The emphasis on primary care development and integration with community health services is similarly prominent. Thus, 'the new NHS' builds on elements of both the internal market and the themes of *Choice and Opportunity*, and brings them more closely together.

Importantly, PMS pilots themselves were to be retained and woven into the new system of PCGs. After a period of reflection, the changes heralded by the Conservative NHS (Primary Care) Act 1997 were described by the Labour Government as 'pioneering'. PCTs (to be created from April 2000) will be able to commission PMS pilots or to act as pilots themselves. Therefore, PMS pilots provide a 'policy bridge' between the historically separate operation of primary care and the long-standing desire for a comprehensive and holistic approach to the planning of health services. PCTs will, for the first time, hold a single budget that may encompass primary, secondary and tertiary care.

What is striking about the recent evolution of health policy in relation to GPs is the degree of consensus between Conservative and Labour governments over the fundamental objectives regarding the management of public resources and the accountability of health professionals. Points of departure focus on policy 'means' rather than policy 'ends'. Both Conservative and Labour governments have acted gradually, to move away from the national GP contract and demand-led funding of GMS while giving GPs greater influence over, but more responsibility for, the wider NHS – thereby avoiding head-on conflict with GPs and the BMA.

Policy implementation

This distinction between means and ends can also be applied to a comparison between the HCHS and GMS policy sectors. While the underlying policy objectives are similar, different means of policy implementation have been preferred. When dealing with general practice, the characteristic feature of recent changes has been that of voluntarism, with new initiatives established as pilot schemes. In primary care, incrementalism rules, with no overt 'masterplan'. *Primary Care: The Future*[34] was explicit about this: 'The government has no preconceived idea about how [development of the role of primary care] can be achieved. Nor are we seeking to impose a single template …'. This contrasts with the more radical and deterministic approach to policy-making that was applied to the HCHS sector – with the wholesale introduction of general management, the 'internal market' and 'the new NHS' representing systemic changes introduced through 'top-down' direction. However, where GPs have directly interfaced with HCHS policy change, voluntary pilots have again been the vehicle of choice (e.g. fundholding, total purchasing pilots and GP commissioning pilots). The fact that all GPs are compelled to join PCGs (albeit at the level of their collective choosing) may represent something of a departure from this incremental, voluntaristic nature of GMS policy evolution.

Policy governing primary medical care provision has, so far, largely avoided the 'big bang' approach to reform and has emerged as the product of many incremental shifts (see Box 2.2).

Box 2.2: POLICY THEMES IN GENERAL MEDICAL SERVICES

Budgetary constraints/incentives

1984 Limited list of GP
pharmaceuticals

1990 Contract
• cash-limiting GMS
• indicative drug budgets

GP fundholding (1991)
• 'real' drug budgets (cash-limited)
• accountability framework (1996)

Total purchasing pilots (1995)

GP commissioning pilots (1997)
• 'real' drug budgets

PMS pilots (1998)
• local contracts for GMS,
  including salaried option
• cash-limiting GMS

The New NHS (1998)
• PCGs
• 'unified budgets' (including GMS
  cash-limited, HCHS and
  prescribing resources), managed
  by GPs and nurses

*Government influence over, and
control of, clinical services*

1984 Limited list of GP
pharmaceuticals

Promoting Better Health (1987) and
Working for Patients (1989)
• pharmaceutical advice to GPs
• audit

1990 Contract
• incentive payments

1997 GMC performance procedures
(professional self-regulation)

PMS pilots (1998)
• local contracts
• salaried practice

The New NHS (1998)
• PCGs
• clinical governance
• NICE & CHImP
• National service frameworks

Conclusion

The role of the GP and, by extension, the national GP contract are now important foci for future health policy development in the NHS. Despite being few in number, PMS pilots now present a significant challenge to the traditional model of primary care. In time, they may be seen as a turning point in the hitherto measured development of primary medical care policy. Notwithstanding the firm Government pledge that the national GP contract will remain an option for those that wish to retain it, its future must now be considered to be in doubt. However, the final destination of policy travel has yet to be determined and the answer to the question, 'who, if anyone, commissions primary care?' is still far from clear.

The Government is eager to promote 'joined up' thinking in health care. By bringing the commissioning and delivery of both primary and secondary care into the ambit of primary care trusts a 'whole systems', or fully integrated, approach to NHS health care is becoming a tantalising possibility.

References

1. Griffiths R. *NHS Management Enquiry*. London: DHSS, 1983.
2. Secretaries of State. *Working for Patients*. London: HMSO, 1989.
3. Butler J. Origins and Early Development. In: Robinson R, Le Grand J, editors. *Evaluating the NHS Reforms*. London: King's Fund Institute, 1994.
4. Le Grand J, Vizard P. The National Health Service: Crisis, Change, or Continuity? In: Glennerster H, Hills J. *The State of Welfare. The Economics of Social Spending*. New York: OUP, 1998.
5. Dixon J. The Context. In: Le Grand J, Mays N, Mulligan J. *Learning from the NHS Internal Market. A review of the evidence*. London: King's Fund Publishing, 1998: 1–14.
6. Packwood T, Keen J, Buxton M. *Hospitals in Transition: the Resource Management Experiment*. Buckingham: Open University Press, 1991.
7. Le Grand J, Mays N, Mulligan J. *Learning from the NHS Internal Market. A review of the evidence*. London: King's Fund Publishing, 1998.
8. Goodwin N. GP fundholding. In: Le Grand J, Mays N, Mulligan J. *Learning from the NHS Internal Market. A review of the evidence*. London: King's Fund Publishing, 1998: 43–68.
9. Dixon J, Holland P, Mays N. Primary care: core values. Developing primary care: gatekeeping, commissioning, and managed care. *British Medical Journal* 1998; 317: 125–28.
10. Glendinning C. GPs and Contracts: Bringing general practice into primary care. *Social Policy and Administration* 1999; 33(2): 115–31.
11. Klein R. *The New Politics of the NHS*. 3rd ed. London: Longman, 1995.
12. Day P. The State, the NHS, and General Practice. *Journal of Public Health Policy* 1992; 13: 165–79.
13. Day P. The State, the NHS, and General Practice. *Journal of Public Health Policy* 1992; 13: 165–79.
14. Lewis J. Primary care – opportunities and threats: The changing meaning of the GP contract. *British Medical Journal* 1997; 314: 895.
15. Langham S, Gillam S, Thorogood M. The carrot, the stick and the general practitioner: how have changes in financial incentives affected health

promotion activity in general practice? *British Journal of General Practice* 1995; 401: 665–68.

16. London Health Planning Consortium. *Primary Health Care in Inner London: Report of a study group* (Chairman Professor ED Acheson). London: DHSS, 1981.

17. Department of Health. *Report of the Inquiry into London's Health Service, Medical Education and Research.* London: HMSO, 1992.

18. Turnberg L. *Health Services in London.* London: Department of Health, 1997.

19. Lewis R. *The London Initiative Zone Review. Moving London's primary care in the right direction.* London: Chief Executives of the 'LIZ' health authorities, 1998.

20. Lewis R. *The London Initiative Zone Review. Moving London's primary care in the right direction.* London: Chief Executives of the 'LIZ' health authorities, 1998.

21. Coulter A, Mays N. Primary care: opportunities and threats. Deregulating primary care. *British Medical Journal* 1997; 314: 510–13.

22. Coulter A, Mays N. Primary care: opportunities and threats. Deregulating primary care. *British Medical Journal* 1997; 314: 510–13.

23. Secretary of State for Health. *Primary care: delivering the future.* London: HMSO, 1996.

24. General Medical Services Committee. *Defining core services in general practice – reclaiming professional control.* London: GMSC, 1996.

25. General Medical Services Committee. *Core services: taking the initiative.* London: GMSC, 1996.

26. British Medical Association General Medical Services Committee. *Medical workforce: task group report.* London: BMA, 1996.

27. NHS Executive. *Patients not paper: report of the efficiency scrutiny in general practice.* Leeds: NHS Executive, 1995.

28. Electoral Reform Ballot Services. *Your choices for the future: a survey of GP opinion, UK report.* London: ERBS, 1992.

29. Secretary of State for Health. *Primary Care: the Future.* Leeds: NHS Executive, 1996.

30. Lewis R, Jenkins C, Gillam S. *Personal Medical Services Pilots in London. Rewriting the Red Book.* London: King's Fund Publishing, 1999.

31. Secretary of State for Health. *The New NHS – Modern, Dependable.* London: HMSO, 1997.

32. NHS Executive. *The New NHS Modern and Dependable. Primary Care Groups: Delivering the Agenda.* Leeds: NHS Executive, 1998.

33. Mays N, Goodwin N. Primary Care Groups in England. In: Klein R, editor. *Implementing the White Paper. Pitfalls and opportunities.* London: King's Fund Publishing, 1998: 1–18.

34. Secretaries of State for Health in England, Wales and Scotland. *Choice and opportunity. Primary care: the future.* London: HMSO, 1996

Chapter 3

Personal Medical Services pilots – new opportunities

Clare Jenkins

KEY POINTS

- Personal Medical Services (PMS) pilot practices were introduced by the NHS (Primary Care) Act 1997

- Becoming a pilot is strictly voluntary, and is seen as being a way to offer innovative new services and experiment with more flexible ways of working

- PMS pilots introduce a number of innovations, including locally negotiated cash-limited contracts and an opportunity for pilot GPs to be salaried. Many of the pilots are managed by trusts, and some are nurse-led

- PMS contracts define the provision of the same range of services as GMS practices, while PMS-plus contracts allow pilots to provide additional services

- PMS pilots were an initiative of the previous government and their place in the policy priority list has varied. PMS pilots are currently heralded as being an important tool for learning to be passed on PCGs and PCTs

- A total of 100 sites formed a first wave of PMS pilots, which went live in April 1998. A further 203 second wave pilots will go live between October 1999 and April 2000

What are Personal Medical Services pilots?

General practice is the main first point of contact with the National Health Service (NHS) – 90 per cent of patient contacts with the NHS occur within primary care.[1] The range of services provided by GPs, known as general medical services (GMS), are governed by the national

GP contract ('the Red Book'[2]), and are defined under regulations found in Part II of the NHS Act 1977. Every resident of the UK has the right to register with a general practitioner (GP) and to have direct access to 24-hour care.

Personal Medical Services (PMS) pilot practices have been created by the NHS (Primary Care) Act 1997 and provide the same broad range of services as traditional GMS practices. However, their legislative lineage is different. Known as PMS pilots simply to differentiate them from GMS practices, sites taking on pilot status transfer from Part II to Part I of the original NHS Act 1977. Part I services (more commonly known as hospital and community health services, or HCHS) have not, until the introduction of PMS pilots, included any element of funding for general practice services.

Becoming a pilot is voluntary, and potential sites submit bids to pilot new approaches to primary care provision, which are then considered by the Secretary of State. If approval is given to 'go live', pilots negotiate their own contracts locally – the first time in 50 years that GPs have been able to work within the NHS but outside the confines of the national GP contract (excluding some specific small-scale schemes discussed in Chapter 6). It is envisaged that the new pilots will be able to respond better to the needs of their local communities by offering innovative new services and experimenting with the skill-mix and organisation of their primary care teams.

The new legislation also allows, for the first time, a range of new providers to become involved in the provision of primary medical care services. Individual nurses and acute and community trusts are now able to submit bids to enter the primary care arena. It was originally mooted that private companies were also to be able to form a PMS pilot, and it was reported that Unichem, BUPA and Healthcall were among seven UK-based private companies interested in the primary care market.[3] However, after disquiet amongst the profession and amidst a flurry of colourful headlines in the popular press,[4] access to NHS contracts was limited to companies that were owned by members of the 'NHS family'.

What makes PMS pilots different?

PMS pilots are required by NHS Executive (NHSE) guidance to provide the same range of services that patients are currently entitled to receive from their GPs under the parallel GMS system[5] – PMS is not a way for practices to 'cherry pick' by providing only one or two selected GMS services. PMS pilots have a number of key characteristics (see Box 3.1).

BOX 3.1: KEY CHARACTERISTICS OF PMS PILOTS

- *Salaried doctors*: since 1948, GPs working within the NHS have enjoyed an 'independent contractor' status, which gives them a high degree of autonomy. However, the enthusiasm for salaried status has increased, particularly amongst younger GPs, for whom the financial implications of owning or renting their own premises and directly employing their own staff are most onerous (see Chapter 6). PMS pilots have introduced, for the first time, the option for GPs to be salaried principals in their own practice, in another practice or a trust

- *New providers*: PMS has allowed a range of new providers to move into the primary care field. Individual nurses, NHS trusts (both acute and community) and private companies were all given the opportunity to enter what had previously been a tightly regulated market, and the medical monopoly was also opened up to a range of other entrants

- *Local contract*: sites taking on PMS pilot status negotiate their contract directly with the health authority. Benefits of using a local contract, rather than the traditional national GP contract, include the ability to tailor services to reflect local needs and circumstances, and to relate incentives and penalties within the contract to meeting quality standards or local priorities

- *Local cash-limit*: the funding for PMS pilots is allocated from the national GP remuneration pool. It forms a separate cash-limit at health authority level and is based on the practices' historical income. The Government has stated that it is 'committed to the principles of achieving equitable distribution of resources, whilst ensuring that GPs who remain in the national contract (under Part II arrangements) will not be disadvantaged nor better off by any pilot-related resource transfers'.[6] However, in practice, PMS contracts use historical expenditure as a guide to the future budget

---

Pilots can take one of two forms, both of which allow the option for GPs to take on salaried status rather than being independent contractors (see Box 3.2).

Box 3.2: 'PMS' OR 'PMS-PLUS'?

- *PMS pilots* provide the broad range of GMS services a patient would expect to receive from any GP, but are cash-limited and operate within a locally specified and negotiated contract

- *PMS-plus pilots* extend the range of services by including non-GMS services such as community nursing, or specialist services such as maternity care, sexual health or services for refugees. This type of pilot has a single contract combining hospital and community health services (HCHS) and GMS funding

---

Uptake of the first wave

The timetable for applications for first wave pilot status was tight – with only 11 months from the preliminary planning stage to actually 'going live':

Table 3.1: Timetable for first wave applications

1 May 1997	Expressions of interest to be with health authorities for forwarding (with comments) to NHSE regional offices
June 1997	Projects notified of whether they were likely to be proceeding to the next stage
June–Oct. 1997	Preparation of detailed applications, including local consultations
1 Nov. 1997	Closing date for applications to the health authority (this date was extended by one month to allow more time for applications)
20 Dec. 1997	Notification of approval by the Secretary of State
Jan.–March 1998	Completion of local preparations
1 April 1998	Pilots established

(Taken from: *Personal Medical Services Pilots under the NHS (Primary Care) Act 1997: a guide to the application and approval process* (NHSE, 1997) and *A guide to Personal Medical Services Pilots under the NHS (Primary Care) Act 1997* (NHSE, 1997).)

The timetable for the second wave is similarly rapid – with only five months from the bids being forwarded to the regional offices by the various health authorities, to going live on 1 October 1999.

Less than a quarter (123/567) of the expressions of interest received from potential primary care providers[7] subsequently became full applications.[8] In December 1997, it was announced that 94 PMS pilots were to be approved,[9, 10] although ultimately there were 95 pilots. A total of 17 pilots given the go-ahead to 'go live' decided not to adopt PMS pilot status, but three additional pilots appeared on a later list from the Department of Health and one pilot split into two separate pilot sites. One pilot, a group of six practices which saw themselves as an embryonic primary care group, went live but gave up PMS pilot status after one year; another site, whose original pilot had not gone ahead, had instead 'gone live' with a separate PMS pilot project.[11] So, of a total of 100 pilots given the go-ahead to 'go live', 17 pilots had failed to get off the ground and one had ceased to operate as a PMS pilot by the end of the first year. With 82 PMS pilots still in operation after one year, this represents an attrition rate of almost 20 per cent (see Table 3.2).

While no limit had been set for the number of PMS pilots that were to enter the first wave, the Department of Health predicted that around one in fourteen (7 per cent) of GP practices would take part.[12] It was expected that subsequent waves would roll out annually, in much the same way as fundholding had previously done. This proved an optimistic calculation and take up of the first wave was smaller than expected. The 83 PMS pilots which actually 'went live' in April 1998 were made up of 127 practices,[13] representing only around 1.3 per cent of all practices in England and Wales.[14] A total of 54 practices made up the 17 PMS pilots that were given the go-ahead to 'go live' but failed to do so.[15] If these practices are included in the calculation, the proportion of PMS pilot practices as a total of the whole is only 1.9 per cent.

Table 3.2: PMS pilots by contract type and provider organisation

	Pilots that 'went live' on 1 April 1998		Pilots that failed to 'go live'	
	No.	%	No.	%
PMS/PMS-plus contract				
PMS only	37	45%	6	35%
PMS-plus	42	51%	11	65%
Not known	4	5%	0	–
Total	83	100%	17	100%
Provider organisation				
Acute trust	1	1%	0	–
Community trust	23	28%	7	41%
Combined trust	2	2%	1	6%
Practice-based	53	64%	9	53%
Practice/community trust partnership	2	2%	0	–
Practice/community trust/ health authority partnership	1	1%	0	–
Not known	1	1%	0	–
Total	83	100%	17	100%

Various reasons can be suggested for the rapid fall-off in numbers of projects expressing an interest in PMS pilot status, to those actually putting together formal bids (Box 3.3).

Box 3.3: REASONS FOR POTENTIAL SITES DECIDING AGAINST SUBMITTING FORMAL PMS PILOT BIDS

- important questions were only slowly resolved. These related to pension rights and the protection offered to Part II GPs, including the 'return ticket' if they decided to withdraw from the PMS pilot

- many proposals submitted did not require the new legislation. Some potential pilots were able to achieve their aims through GMS local development schemes

- PMS pilots attracted opposition from the medical profession and the press carried hostile stories

- the new health policy of the incoming Labour Government and the announcement of primary care groups (PCGs) soon overshadowed the NHS (Primary Care) Act 1997

PMS-plus pilot sites were more likely to fail to 'go live' than straight PMS sites. This may have been due to the difficulties involved in drawing up a PMS-plus contract, with additional services specified, and in such short timescales, or simply to the overall complexity of this type of project.

Around two-thirds of PMS pilot sites that 'went live' were practice-based, the other third were trust-based. The majority of trust-based pilots were proposed by community trusts, although two were combined acute and community trust managed, and one was set up by an acute trust. Proportionately more trust-based pilots failed to go live, for reasons given below (see Box 3.4). This is not surprising as trust-based pilots were, in many cases, setting practices up from scratch, using PMS-plus contracts, and were based in more deprived areas (see Chapter 4). The difficulties involved and the steep learning curves encountered in setting up new practices have been graphically described by trust-based pilots.[16]

BOX 3.4: REASONS GIVEN BY PMS PILOTS FOR THEIR DECISION NOT TO 'GO LIVE'

- disagreement between the pilot and the health authority over funding
- the difficulty of getting complex projects off the ground in the short timescales given
- health authority resistance to pilot projects in their area
- difficulties in finalising local contracts
- objectives of the pilot were now achievable through the new PCG
- difficulties in appointing suitable GP candidates

Resistance to wave 1

Although the NHS (Primary Care) Act 1997 was introduced to improve provision of both the range and quality of primary care services, particularly for marginalised populations, PMS pilots were not universally welcomed. Despite the assurances of the Government that independent contractor status would remain for those GPs who wanted it,[17] the salaried option was seen by many as being 'the thin end of the wedge', leading, in the long term, to all GPs becoming directly managed and salaried NHS staff. It was suggested that the ability of GPs to prescribe and refer in the best interests of their patients, and to comment on standards of care and levels of provision in their area might be compromised by any changed employment status.[18] With fewer GPs working within GMS, the powers of the GP national negotiating body could be weakened, and the national pool of money from which GPs are paid potentially reduced.[19] The popular press forecast that PMS pilots would lead to the demise of the Red Book[20] and, locally, pilots reported suspicion from neighbouring practices who viewed the pilots as a possible threat to their list sizes.

Despite the storm of negative headlines that appeared in the professional press throughout the latter part of 1996 and the early part of 1997, the situation seemed to calm quite rapidly. The PMS pilots 'went live' in April 1998 quietly and without great publicity. This was partly due to the process of agreeing boundaries for the new PCGs, which diverted attention away from PMS pilots. As new pilots have become known to local practices, the antagonism that they initially felt has diminished.

Prospects for the second wave

PMS pilots, a brainchild of the Major Government, have waxed and waned in terms of their policy importance to the current administration. PMS pilots are now more visible again. Alan Milburn, former Health Minister, described them as a 'win-win plan for primary care'[21] and they are now viewed as offering a valuable opportunity for learning to be passed on to PCGs and, in particular, primary care trusts (PCTs). Guidance for the second wave[22] described six specific areas where PMS pilots can contribute to the development of PCGs and PCTs (see Box 3.5).

BOX 3.5: AREAS WHERE PMS PILOTS CAN PROVIDE LEARNING FOR PCGS AND PCTS

- to test out organisational models and behaviour prior to moving to a different level of PCG

- to test out the move to a locally targeted contract

- to test out shared management arrangements and to experiment with skill-mix

- to tackle specific problems affecting the delivery of primary care services

- to tackle specific local health problems

- to play a full role in shaping their local Health Improvement Programme (HImP)

PMS pilots will be expected to work closely with their PCG – playing a full part in its activities and fitting in with its organisational structures – and the consistency of the PMS pilots' aims with the service objectives of the PCG will be a major factor in the Secretary of State's decision on whether to give a pilot the go-ahead. PMS pilots will also need to participate in local clinical governance arrangements and be consistent with the objectives of the HImP.[23]

A total of 171 new PMS pilots, due to go live on 1 October 1999, were announced in July by the Secretary of State for Health, Frank Dobson,[24] with a further 32 pilots added in September 1999,[25] which will go live by April 2000. These new sites more than treble the total number of PMS pilots across the country, and increase the proportion of health authorities who have one or more PMS pilots within their area from just over half (52 per cent) to four out of five (80 per cent). The characteristics of the second wave pilots differ somewhat from those of the first wave. Most of the new pilots are practice-based (87 per cent), and the majority of these are single-practice sites. The remainder of pilots are made up of trust-managed sites and partnerships between practices and trusts. In the first wave, almost a third of pilots were trust-based. Increases in PMS pilot numbers have been much more significant in some parts of the country, particularly the south, than in others (see Chapter 4).

The role of evaluation

The Government has stipulated that when sites become PMS pilots, they must evaluate the work they are undertaking at both a local and national level.[26] Local evaluations, carried out either independently or in collaboration with other research organisations, are likely to be formative, helping shape the local health economy. The centrally funded national evaluation is being co-ordinated by the National Primary Care Research and Development Centre (NPCRDC).[27] The national evaluation is a summative evaluation carried out over the three years of the pilots' lives, and is made up of four separate studies. It addresses strategic policy issues by analysing the characteristics and experiences of all the PMS pilot sites. The aim of both the national and local evaluations is to review the learning emerging from the PMS pilots, before any decision is made concerning their long-term future.

References

1. Department of Health. *Primary care: the future*. London: NHSE, 1996.
2. Department of Health/Welsh Office. *National Health Service General Medical Services: Statement of fees and allowances payable to general medical practitioners in England and Wales*.
3. Stirling A. Private firms eager to snap up primary care. *Pulse* 1996; 56(49): 2–3.
4. Stirling A. Private firms scent GP bonanza. *Pulse* 1996; 56(49): 1.
5. Department of Health. *Personal Medical Services Pilots under the NHS (Primary Care) Act 1997: a comprehensive guide*. London: NHSE, 1997.
6. Department of Health. *Personal Medical Services Pilots under the NHS (Primary Care) Act 1997: a comprehensive guide*. London: NHSE, 1997.
7. Department of Health press release 97/151. Alan Milburn announces Primary Care Act pilots. 1 July 1997.
8. Leeds: NHSE, 11 November 1998 (personal communication).
9. Department of Health press release 97/416. New pilots will improve quality in primary care services. 23 December 1997.
10. It is difficult to ascertain exact numbers of PMS pilots at each stage of the bidding process as data sources vary in the numbers given.
11. The King's Fund contacted the project leads at all 95 PMS pilots in April and May 1999 to ask whether their projects had 'gone live', currently remained 'live' and whether the number of participating practices had changed during the first year of operation.
12. Elliot A. Dorrell lights the GP fuse. *Pulse* 1996; 56(44): 1.

13. Number of practices as at April 1999. One pilot is not based in a practice, but involves a team of GPs employed by an acute trust.
14. The number of practices in England and Wales in 1996 was 9561: Jones R, Menzies S. *General Practice essential facts*. Abingdon: Radcliffe Medical Press, 1999.
15. Number of practices as at December 1997.
16. Lewis R, Jenkins C, Gillam S. *Personal Medical Services pilots in London: rewriting the Red Book*. London: King's Fund Publishing, 1999.
17. NHS Executive. *Primary Care Trusts: Establishing better services*. London: Department of Health, 1999.
18. Heath I. Threat to social justice. *British Medical Journal* 1997; 314: 598.
19. Lewis R, Jenkins C. A quiet revolution in primary care. *Guardian (Society)*. In press.
20. Ministers sound Red Book's death knell. *Pulse* 1996; 56(30): 1.
21. Milburn A. General practice and the New NHS. Speech at Royal College of General Practitioners, 7 October 1998.
22. Department of Health. *Personal Medical Services pilots under the NHS (Primary Care) Act 1997. A comprehensive guide – second edition*. London: NHSE, 1998.
23. Department of Health. *Personal Medical Services pilots under the NHS (Primary Care) Act 1997. A comprehensive guide – second edition*. London: NHSE, 1998.
24. Department of Health press release 99/0447. New boost for better primary as number of trailblazing pilots triples. 16 July 1999.
25. Department of Health press release 99/0520. 32 new pilots takes total to nearly 300: additional personal medical services pilots announced. 1 September 1999.
26. Department of Health. *Personal Medical Services pilots under the NHS (Primary Care) Act 1997, a guide to local evaluation*. London: NHSE, 1997.
27. Leese B, Gosden T, Riley A, Allen L and Campbell S. *Setting out: Piloting innovations in primary care. Report on behalf of PMS National Evaluation Team*. Manchester: NPCRDC, 1999.

Chapter 4

Reducing inequality

Clare Jenkins and Richard Lewis

KEY POINTS

- There are well-recognised variations in health related to socio-economic status and place of residence. The geographical distribution of GPs remains uneven

- PMS pilots were launched as a means of introducing more flexibility into underserved areas, such as the inner city, where population needs are highest

- PMS pilots are not equally distributed across the country. They are more likely to be found in inner city, urban, mining and industrial areas than in prosperous and rural areas

- First wave PMS pilot practices are based in more deprived electoral wards than are English practices overall, and this is particularly true of trust-based and nurse-led pilots

- Many of the pilots have set out to address the specific needs of particularly marginalised populations such as asylum seekers, refugees, the homeless and drug users

- It is too early yet to say how far PMS pilots have succeeded in reducing inequality amongst the populations they serve

Introduction

The existence of social and geographical variations in the health of the British population is well recognised. A person's socio-economic status is likely to affect their well-being – health, on average, is worse for the relatively deprived. Levels of ill health are higher, on average, in inner city areas than in suburban or rural areas, and mortality rates in the north and west of Britain are higher than in the south.[1] Such long-standing inequalities in the nation's health, which were described in the Black Report[2] and reaffirmed in the recent Acheson Report,[3] remain a major policy issue which successive governments have sought to address.[4,5] However, over the last two decades, although prosperity has increased and national mortality rates have fallen, inequalities in health between the rich and the poor have widened. The White Paper *Choice and Opportunity*[6] and guidance issued in support of PMS pilots have stressed the importance of the pilots' contribution to tackling inequalities.

In the same way that mortality and morbidity varies across the country, so does the distribution of general practitioner (GP) services relative to need. Although the work of the Medical Practices Committee has influenced the distribution of GPs, areas with the greatest needs remain underserved.[7,8] In areas where needs are greatest, such as the inner city, service provision and infrastructure tend to be poorer.[9,10,11] List sizes are large and general practitioners are more likely to be the only practice GP and be older than the national average. There are problems with staff recruitment and morale may be low. Such characteristics of primary care in deprived areas add to the specific needs of populations for which population mobility, homelessness and poverty are also an issue.[12] Finally, marginalised groups have difficulty registering with a GP.[13,14]

There are a number of reasons for the apparent mismatch between population need and primary care provision. Practices in inner city and deprived areas are more likely to experience problems in recruiting for general practice vacancies,[15] but not necessarily in retaining young GPs once appointed.[16] Structural factors such as the expense of property, both practice and residential, as well as lack of space, traffic congestion and fear of violence have a role to play in making the inner city a less desirable place for new GPs to work.[17] High patient mobility makes target payments based on population coverage difficult to achieve and capitation payments provide an incentive for large patient lists, notwithstanding the high demand for care. Traditional means of investing in primary care premises have proved inadequate in dealing with long-standing deficits in London's primary care capital stock.[18]

The crisis in recruitment in deprived areas will deepen as a large number of GPs who qualified in south Asia reach retirement age within the next ten years,[19] and as the popularity of general practice as a career choice for recently qualified doctors appears to be falling.[20] While the number of doctors becoming full-time unrestricted principals has declined, the numbers choosing to work part-time have increased.[21]

Prior to the introduction of PMS pilots, a number of attempts had been made to address the apparent deficiencies of the GP contract in meeting the needs of the disadvantaged. These attempts included the general reform of the system of remuneration as well as the development of small scale schemes designed to fill the gaps left by the national system. The former is exemplified by the introduction of 'deprivation payments' made available to GPs for each of their patients who lived in an electoral ward with high 'Jarman scores'. The underprivileged area score (UPA) is a scaling system based on a range of characteristics that GPs felt to be associated with high workload. However, the payments have been criticised for lack of sensitivity as well as for favouring the inner city while failing to take account of rural poverty. [22,23,24] There have been many calls for deprivation payments to be based on enumeration districts[25] as a means of improving the sensitivity of the system, a change that is currently being implemented.

Other limited schemes have been developed to address particular problems with the provision of primary care. The Secretary of State has discretion under section 56 of the NHS Act 1977 to authorise the employment of salaried doctors, and a range of schemes were adopted, in particular to serve homeless populations. The London Initiative Zone (LIZ) development programme funded an extensive range of targeted schemes for ethnic minorities and homeless people[26] as well as a new cadre of GP assistants. The NHS (Primary Care) Act 1997 also introduced flexibility within GMS to enable local development schemes to fund enhanced primary care services, one purpose of which was to address those needs not adequately met by mainstream services. This mirrored a pilot project undertaken in one London health authority that involved direct incentives through a fee for service to enhance the primary care of people with severe mental illness.[27]

Location of PMS pilots in England

The location of first wave PMS pilots is uneven across the country. Of the 82 PMS pilots that remained in operation at the end of year one, the majority (59 per cent, 48) were in the north and midlands. In the south of the country, there were 34 pilots, the majority of which (77 per cent, 26) were in London (see Table 4.1). Large areas of the country such as Devon and Cornwall and East Anglia have no first wave pilots at all.

Table 4.1: Distribution of first wave PMS pilots by region

Regional office	No. of PMS pilots
Trent	9
North west	13
Northern and Yorkshire	14
West Midlands	12
South Thames	14
North Thames	12
Anglia and Oxford	2
South and west	6
Total	82

The remainder of this Chapter considers how far in its first year the uptake of PMS – a policy explicitly designed to introduce local flexibility, particularly in underserved areas – has been located in areas where need is greatest. Two data sources have been used to analyse the location of PMS pilots. First, the Office of National Statistics (ONS) area classification[28] has been used to classify the health authority areas in which the PMS pilots were sited. Secondly, underprivileged area scores[29, 30] for the electoral wards within which the PMS pilots were located have been used to provide a more detailed level of analysis.

Location of PMS pilots by ONS area classification

The ONS area classification system provides an indicator of the characteristics of health authority and local authority areas for comparative purposes. The classification measures similarities across a whole range of variables, grouping similar areas into clusters and using six classification 'families'.

Of the 100 health authority areas in England, just over half (52 per cent) had one or more PMS pilot projects within their area. Table 4.2 shows the distribution of PMS pilots by ONS health authority classification. The largest numbers of pilots were located in health authority areas with an 'urban' classification (urban centres and inner London). Almost a quarter of pilots were located in mining and industrial areas, with almost one in five in maturer areas. The smallest numbers of pilots were found in prospering and rural areas.

Table 4.2: Distribution of HA areas within ONS area classification for England

ONS family	First wave PMS pilots	
	No.	%
Inner London	6	7
Maturer areas	15	18
Mining/industrial areas	20	24
Prospering areas	13	16
Rural areas	9	11
Urban centres	19	23
Total	82	99

Clearly, the characteristics of the health authority population overall may not reflect those of the PMS practice population. For example, Oxfordshire is classified as a 'prospering' area, while its PMS pilot, based in central Oxford, is targetting its services at the homeless.

Underprivileged area scores

First wave PMS pilots can also be analysed using UPA scores. The following analysis of deprivation scores has been based on the 80 PMS pilots which remain live after their first full year of operation and for whom practice postcodes were available. Postcodes were used to link practice location to individual electoral wards, whose populations are generally around 5000 people. The 1991 census returns, on which the current ward data are based, have been criticised because of the problems associated with under-enumeration. They are also now almost ten years out of date. Two pilots were omitted from the analysis: one pilot was based in an acute trust and not a practice, and the other was unable to provide a postcode as it had been developed on a green field site, which did not have an allocated postcode prior to 1998. Mean deprivation scores were calculated for the 15 pilots with more than one participating practice. There are clearly limitations associated with attributing ward data to practice populations. However, this method has been used in preference to calculating practice population based deprivation scores because many pilots had only been registering patients for a few months and had small list sizes, which may be unrepresentative of their later populations.

Nationally, 5 per cent of wards attract a payment, and UPA scores range from around minus 50, in the most prosperous areas, to about plus 70 in the most deprived of areas. Because of standardisation, the mean score is zero. Table 4.3 shows the mean UPA scores for groups of PMS pilots.

Table 4.3: Underprivileged area scores by type of PMS pilot

Type of Pilot	No.	Mean UPA score	Range UPA scores Min.	Max.
All English wards	8595	0.00	−44.95	68.49
All PMS pilots	80	12.33	−19.47	62.01
Practice-based pilots	53	9.90	−17.18	62.01
Community trust-based pilots	22	16.46	−19.47	56.67
Nurse-led/nurse-partnership pilots	9	18.83	−10.28	31.86

Of the 30 most underprivileged health authority areas in the country, 22 (73 per cent) have PMS pilots within their areas, whereas only 13 (43 per cent) of the 30 least underprivileged health authorities have PMS pilots. The difference between overall health authority UPA scores and PMS pilot UPA scores was calculated. On average, the ward UPA scores for the PMS pilots was 9.05 points higher than the overall score for the health authority in which the pilot was based. From these results, it would appear that PMS pilots are sited in more deprived areas, and this is particularly true for nurse-led/nurse-partnership and trust-based pilots. PMS pilots are also more likely to be situated in more deprived areas within their health authority boundary. One of the four studies making up the national PMS pilots evaluation (see Chapter 3) will be carrying out a more detailed socio-geographic analysis of the PMS pilots and their target populations.[31]

The second wave

A total of 171 second wave PMS pilots were announced in July 1999, with a further 32 added to the list in September 1999. Almost two-thirds of the new pilots are situated in the south of the country, whereas 42 per cent of the first wave were within the new London, south east, eastern and south west region boundaries.

Some regions will see the numbers of PMS pilots increase markedly when the new pilots go live in October 1999. The most striking increase will be seen in the London region, where a total of 58 new pilots have been announced. Even if the rate of attrition of the second wave pilots mirrors that of the first wave (around 20 per cent), the number of PMS pilots in the capital is set to quadruple. In one inner London health authority area, 28 new pilots have been announced, to join the four PMS pilots already in operation there. The number of PMS pilots is set to more than treble in the south east (29 second wave pilots were announced, compared with 11 in the first wave), and there are also significant increases in the south west region (seven pilot sites were announced in the first wave, and 20 in the second wave).

The following table shows the numbers of new PMS pilots by ONS area classification. Increases were most noticeable in inner London, in prospering areas and also in rural areas. It appears that second wave PMS pilots are more likely than first wave pilots to be found in the south of the country, to be practice-based, and to be based in single practices (see Chapter 3). With the second wave, PMS pilots have increased markedly in inner London, but also in the less deprived health authority areas overall. While classification by health authority area is likely to tell us little about the socio-economic characteristics of the individual pilot populations, these initial findings suggest that second wave pilots may differ as a group from those of the first wave.

Table 4.4: Second wave PMS pilots by ONS area classification

ONS category (Based on health authority boundaries.)	First wave No.	Second wave No.	% increase/ decrease in number of pilots
Inner London	7	32	457% increase
Maturer areas	20	39	195% increase
Mining and industrial areas	26	41	158% increase
Prospering areas	15	47	313% increase
Rural areas	9	22	244% increase
Urban centres	23	22	96% increase
Total	100	203	203% increase

Reducing inequalities in different areas

Guidance issued for first wave PMS pilot sites made it clear that PMS pilots were to focus on local service problems and bring about improvements in primary care provision by using different ways of delivering services.[32] The introduction of PMS pilots may reduce inequality in the following ways:

• providing a service where none exists
• increasing the quality of care where local primary care may be poor
• targetting the needs of specific populations
• as a vehicle for channelling additional resources not available via the national contracting mechanism.

Although PMS pilots were intended to improve services in areas where the quality of primary care was poor, the initiative was not geographically restricted. While pilots have been set up in the most deprived of inner city areas, such as Toxteth, Salford, Lambeth and Tower Hamlets, they have also been used to provide services in a range of other locations.

Examples of PMS pilots

In Isleworth, west London, a new primary care centre was set up in an area where a growing population and the closure of primary care facilities meant that patients were finding it increasingly difficult to register with a local practice. The project was a collaboration between Ealing,

Hammersmith and Hounslow health authority and Hounslow and Spelthorne community and mental health trust. A team of two GPs, a nurse practitioner and a range of other health care professionals now work at the new surgery to provide a comprehensive range of primary care services. Although patient registrations have now levelled off, in the first few months of operation up to 80 new patients were registering every week.

In Toxteth, an inner city area of Liverpool, a PMS pilot was set up in association with Liverpool health authority and North Mersey community (NHS) trust. It was planned that the pilot, based in an inner city practice in Liverpool, with a team of six GPs and a comprehensive primary health care team, would become a new primary care provider directorate within the community trust. The aims of the pilot include an emphasis on working in partnership with local statutory and voluntary agencies, increasing accessibility for all groups of local people, and attracting and retaining high quality health professionals.

Conclusion

Urban and inner city practices often lag behind practices in suburban and rural areas in the uptake of new initiatives.[33] PMS pilots, which are more likely to be found in deprived areas than more prosperous ones, appear to contradict this finding. The first wave of PMS pilots were most likely to be initiated 'bottom-up' by the projects themselves, rather than by health authorities.[34] In future, primary care groups (PCGs) will be able to take a more top-down approach and commission pilots in areas where they identify greatest need.

The first wave of PMS pilots are situated in areas with higher levels of deprivation. They are more likely to be found in inner London, in mining and industrial areas, and in urban areas; they are less likely to be found in prospering and rural areas. This is particularly the case for trust-based and 'nurse-led' pilots. Practice-based pilots are more likely to be in more affluent areas than trust-based pilots, but they are still targetting more deprived populations than the average practice.

The development of a PMS pilot in an area of high need (or any other area) does not necessarily mean that high quality services will be provided from the start – however enthusiastic the pilot staff are.

PMS pilots have set out with ambitious aims. In addition, the desire of PMS pilots to register patients with particular needs or from particular groups may not itself be sufficient to achieve that outcome. Establishing whether these pilots have achieved the aims they have set themselves will be the task of the local and national evaluations.

References

1. Curtis S. Geographical perspectives on poverty, health and health policy in different parts of the UK. In: Philo C, editor. *Off the Map, the social geography of poverty in the UK*. London: Child Poverty Action Group, 1995.
2. Black D, Morris JN, Smith C, Townsend P. *Inequalities in health: report of a research working group*. London: Department of Health and Social Security, 1980 (The Black Report).
3. Acheson D. *Independent inquiry into inequalities in health*. London: Stationery Office, 1998 (The Acheson Report).
4. Secretary of State for Health. *The health of the nation: a strategy for health in England*. London: Stationery Office, 1992.
5. Secretary of State for Health. *Our healthier nation: a contract for health*. London: Stationery Office, 1998.
6. Secretary of State for Health. *Choice and opportunity: primary care, the future*. London: The Stationery Office, 1996.
7. Benzeval M, Judge K. Access to health care in England: continuing inequalities in the distribution of GPs. *Journal of Public Health Medicine* 1996; 18(1): 33–40.
8. Gravelle H, Sutton M. Trends in geographical inequalities in provision of general practitioners in England and Wales. *Lancet* 1998; 352: 1910.
9. Boyle S, Hamblin R. *The health economy of London: a report to the King's Fund London Commission*. London: King's Fund Publishing, 1997.
10. Turnberg L. *Health services in London – a strategic review*. London: Department of Health, 1998.
11. Lewis R. *London Initiative Zone Review. Moving London's primary care in the right direction. Report on behalf of the Chief Executives of the 'LIZ' Health Authorities*. London: Waldon and White, 1998.
12. Pringle M. Primary Care: opportunities and threats: distributing primary care fairly. *British Medical Journal* 1997; 314: 595.
13. Jones D, Gill PS. Refugees and primary care: tackling the inequalities. *British Medical Journal* 1998; 317: 1444–46.
14. Hinton T. Researching homelessness and access to health care. *Critical Public Health* 1994; 5(3): 33–38.
15. Carlisle R, Johnstone S. Factors influencing the response to advertisements for general practice vacancies. *British Medical Journal* 1996; 313: 468–71.

16. Taylor DH, Quayle JA, Roberts C. Retention of young general practitioners entering the NHS from 1991–1992. *British Journal of General Practice* 1999; 49: 277–80.

17. Harris T, Silver T, Rink E, Hilton S. Vocational training for general practice in inner London. Is there a dearth? And if so what's to be done? *British Medical Journal* 1996; 312: 97–101.

18. Lewis R. *Review of primary care capital development in light of the LIZ experience.* Leeds: NHS Estates, 1998.

19. Taylor DH, Esmail A. Retrospective analysis of census data on general practitioners who qualified in South Asia: who will replace them as they retire? *British Medical Journal* 1999; 318: 306–10.

20. Lambert TW, Goldacre MJ, Edwards C, Parkhouse J. Career preferences of doctors who qualified in the United Kingdom in 1993 compared with those of doctors qualifying in 1974, 1977, 1980 and 1983. *British Medical Journal* 1996; 313: 19–24.

21. Taylor DH, Leese B. Recruitment, retention, and time commitment change of general practitioners in England and Wales, 1990–94: a retrospective study. *British Medical Journal* 1997; 314: 1806.

22. O'Reilly D, Steele K. More equitable systems for allocating general practice deprivation payments: financial consequences. *British Journal of General Practice* 1998; 48: 1405–07.

23. Cox J. Rural general practice: a personal view of current key issues. *Health Bulletin* 1997; 55(5): 309–15.

24. Rousseau N, McColl E, Eccles M. *Primary health care in rural areas: issues of equity and resource management – a literature review.* Newcastle upon Tyne: Centre for Health Services Research, 1994.

25. Hobbs R and Cole T. Deprivation payments revisited (again). *British Medical Journal* 1996; 313: 641–42.

26. Lewis R. *The London Initiative Zone Review. Moving London's primary care in the right direction.* London: Chief Executives of the 'LIZ' Health Authorities, 1998.

27. Burns T, Cohen A. Item-of-service payments for general practitioner care of severely mentally ill persons: does the money matter? *British Journal of General Practice* 1998; 48(432): 1415–16.

28. Wallace M, Denham C. *The ONS classification of local and health authorities of Great Britain.* Office for National Statistics. London: HMSO, 1996.

29. Jarman B. Identification of underprivileged areas. *British Medical Journal* 1983; 286: 1705–09.

30. Jarman B. Underprivileged areas: validation and distribution of scores. *British Medical Journal* 1984; 289: 1587–92.

31. 'National evaluation of Primary Care Act pilots – addressing inequalities' is being carried out by a team led by Professor Yvonne Carter at Queen Mary and Westfield College, London.

32. Department of Health. *Personal Medical Services pilots under the NHS (Primary Care) Act 1997: a comprehensive guide.* London: NHSE, 1997.
33. Leese B, Bosanquet N. Change in general practice and its effects on service provision in areas with different socio-economic characteristics. *British Medical Journal* 1995; 311: 546–50.
34. Lewis R, Jenkins C, Gillam S. *Personal Medical Services pilots in London: rewriting the Red Book.* London: King's Fund Publishing, 1999.

Chapter 5

Nurse-led PMS pilots

Diane Jones

KEY POINTS

- The number of nurses in primary care has increased substantially over the last 30 years and their role has changed significantly with the introduction of nurse practitioners and nurse prescribing

- PMS pilots have increased the opportunities for nurses and ten pilots are 'nurse-led'

- There are three models of 'nurse-led' pilots: the nurse as independent contractor, the nurse as lead professional salaried by a community trust, and the nurse as an equal partner

- Nurse-led pilots have faced a range of challenges in implementing their projects, including administrative obstacles, restricted prescribing rights, human resources issues and acceptance by GPs

- A key question for evaluation is whether this model of care is cost-effective and sustainable and therefore able to assist with the problems of recruitment and retention of GPs

Background

Nurses have played a role within general practice since 1911,[1] although nurse attachments to general practice were not reported until the 1950s.[2] From the outset their role included not only nursing duties but also reception and administrative work. There was often no contract of employment or formal job description and no formal educational preparation[3] for this role.

In 1966 the partial reimbursement of practice staff salaries (including practice nurses) was introduced via the Family Doctors' Charter,[4, 5] and at the time it was estimated that there were 244 full-time practice nurses in England and Wales.[6] By 1985 this figure had risen to 4500. Over the next nine years there was a fourfold increase in the number of nurses in general practice, so that in 1994 the number was estimated to be approximately 17,500.[7]

The reimbursement of 70 per cent of the cost of employing practice staff played a major part in the initial growth of nurses in general practice, especially as nurses could undertake some of the routine work which had previously been completed by GPs. The 1990 GP contract was a major catalyst for the substantial growth in numbers of practice nurses as it introduced payment for various health promoting activities undertaken by nurses.

A further development in primary care nursing has been the introduction of nurse practitioners. The role was first piloted in the UK in the 1980s, having originated in the USA in the 1960s.[8] They developed in the UK in response to deficits in health care provision, often working with underserved groups in inner city communities such as homeless people.[9] By 1990 the Royal College of Nursing had developed formal training for nurse practitioners and, ultimately, a degree course. Through the 1990s increases in the number of nurse practitioners have been slow in Britain compared with the USA.[10]

The role of the nurse practitioner has been defined as 'an advanced level clinical nurse who through extra education and training, is able to practice autonomously, making clinical decisions and instigating treatments based on those decisions, and is fully accountable for her own practice'.[11] This extension to the nursing role includes skills which are normally associated with GPs – including clinical assessment, diagnosis, treatment and, to a degree at least, prescribing. These responsibilities cross the traditional boundaries between medicine and nursing.[12]

A further development was the introduction of nurse prescribing, which was piloted from 1994 to 1998 and is now to be rolled out across England.[13] However, the list of items a nurse can prescribe is limited to little more than medicines that are available over the counter. This allows suitably qualified nurses to prescribe the types of items they often need without calling upon a GP, but for a nurse-led pilot this list may be far too limited.

The NHS (Primary Care) Act 1997

Within this context, it is not surprising that nurses would seek alternative models of providing primary care under the 1997 Act. However, when the White Papers *Choice and Opportunity*[14] and *Delivering the Future*[15] were published there were scant references to nursing and few people envisaged the way in which nurse-led PMS pilots would develop. In July 1997, when the first expressions of interest were analysed, the number submitted by nurses was negligible. At this point the Health Minister, Alan Milburn, stated that the Government was 'particularly keen to see plans being developed by nurses, working with GPs, to bring forward their own ideas on how the full range of primary care services can be improved'.[16] The professional bodies representing nursing welcomed this and worked with individual nurses and other nursing bodies to encourage involvement.

Eight first wave sites were deemed to be nurse-led. In two the nurse is an independent contractor and in six the nurses are based within a community trust. This figure can be increased to ten by including schemes where the nurse is accepted as an equal partner of the GP.[17] As nurse-led pilots had not been clearly envisaged at the beginning of the process, little thought had been given to the practical issues surrounding nurse-led or nurse-partner pilots. The emerging challenges faced by nurse-led pilots are considered in this Chapter.

Types of nurse-led pilot

There is no clear understanding of what is meant by a nurse-led PMS pilot. The use of the term 'nurse-led' implies that power has shifted from the GP to the nurse. In practice, however, many of the pilots have focused upon developing democratic consensus and professional respect, where the needs of patients are matched to the skills of the practitioner.

Three types of nurse-led pilot have emerged:

1. Nurse as an independent contractor

Within this model the nurse becomes the independent contractor who holds a contract with the health authority to provide personal medical services. The nurse then contracts with a GP to provide medical cover on a sessional or salaried basis.

The lead nurse is self-employed in a similar manner to an independent contractor GP. The nurse is therefore responsible for the organisation and management of the practice, including management of finances and premises and the employment of staff.

There are only two pilots of this nature, based at Salford and southern Derbyshire. At the southern Derbyshire pilot the lead nurse employs the reception staff, practice manager, GP and the nurse. The community nurses remain employed by the community trust. At the Salford pilot the lead nurse employs the GP and the reception staff. All other nursing staff are employed by the local community trust as the lead nurse felt it was not appropriate to employ nurses.

The contract between the HA and the lead nurse contains targets similar to those in the GP contract. However, under PMS it is possible to be more flexible, allowing more appropriate targets to be set. Furthermore, under PMS an annual budget is set, so that if the practice fails to meet a target, the payment remains the same until the budget is renegotiated the following year.

2. Nurse as lead professional salaried by a community trust

In this model all staff within the pilot are salaried by a community trust. The lead nurse acts as the team leader and is accountable for the development of services within the practice. The lead nurse also undertakes the primary assessment and management of patients, only referring the patient to a GP if necessary.

Lambeth Health Care NHS Trust is currently undertaking such a pilot at the Edith Cavell practice. The Trust believes that once the pilot is fully established, with more nurses on the team, 'between 50% and 60% of contacts could be managed entirely by a member of the nursing team'[18] – therefore greatly reducing the need for GP services. The expertise of the salaried GP would then be focused upon the management of more complicated cases, the development of care pathways and also the application of evidence-based health care. One of the major benefits of community trust involvement is the range of expertise that the trust can bring to the pilot, including information management and technology, human resources, financial and estates management.

3. Nurse as an equal partner

This third model is not really nurse-led but involves the nurse and the GP as equal partners. Whereas the nurse-led models focus upon the nurse as the initial point of contact, this model has multiple initial points of contact.

The pilot managed by Warrington Community Health NHS Trust has employed a salaried GP, two nurse practitioners and a primary care nurse. Other professionals are also involved, such as child health specialists and physiotherapists. Patients may therefore choose to see a GP, a nurse practitioner or the primary care nurse as their first point of contact. Prior to registering with the practice the different skills and abilities of each of the practitioners is explained to the patient.

Clinical responsibility lies with each individual clinician. However, the team has a management board consisting of the GP, nurse practitioner and project manager. The GP takes responsibility for medical matters, the nurse practitioner for nursing issues and the project manager takes overall responsibility for the pilot. A genuinely multidisciplinary team of equal status was an attractive proposition for health care professionals (as evidenced by the level and quality of candidates seeking work in the pilot). More importantly, patients should benefit from access to a wider range of skills.

Common challenges for nurse-led PMS

As nurse-led pilots were not anticipated when the NHS (Primary Care) Act was developed, implementation has been problematic in several ways.

Administrative/management issues

There are several areas in which managing a nurse-led site is complicated. First, all patients must be registered with a GP. This implies that the GP would have some form of liability towards the patient but may have no clinical relationship with them.

Furthermore, having to register patients with a GP could undermine nurse-led pilots in various ways. It implies that ultimate responsibility lies with a GP (which is difficult if the only contact the patient has had is with a nurse) and it reinforces the subservience of nurse to doctor.

One solution has been to register patients with the salaried GP attached to the practice. This has proved workable in practice but if, in the future, the pilots become permanent, other ways of registering patients need to be considered. This may include registering patients with the practice as a whole, as some general practices already do.

The Mental Health Act 1993 presents a further problem for nurse-led sites. Under the Act, an approved social worker and a responsible medical officer (which includes psychiatrists or sometimes a GP) must sign section documentation. There is, however, no provision for a nurse to sign the section documentation (although under section 5(4) hospital nurses can delay the discharge of a patient). This is problematic for nurse-led pilots as it means that they must find a responsible medical officer and a social worker.

Nurses are not allowed to certify death in any circumstances although they may confirm death. Nurses do not qualify as attending clinicians prior to a sudden death. All sudden deaths within a nurse-led pilot therefore require a post mortem if the patient has only consulted with the nurse. This is inappropriate and adds further stress to families of the deceased.

Information systems and information technology also raise different issues for nurse-led pilots. Practice-based clinical systems have been developed to fulfil the requirements of GP-led practices and existing systems can be a problem for nurse-led pilots. Information management and technology in PMS pilots is explored further in Chapter 8.

Prescribing

Nurse-led PMS pilots were not originally given any additional powers to prescribe. In Salford, for example, the lead nurse, who has completed the nurse prescribing course, has not been allowed to prescribe from the limited list. One solution to this problem would be for the GP to use a modem connection to send a prescription directly to a pharmacy from a remote computer. However, under the Medicines Act 1973 all prescriptions must be signed by hand in ink, by the medical practitioner – and so far this remains unchanged.

The guidance for second wave PMS schemes states that the regulations governing nurse prescribing are likely to be extended – a matter of urgency for nurse-led pilots.

Human resources issues

Nurse-led PMS pilots raise several questions relating to staff recruitment. For example, what is the right kind of nurse for the post, and what skills should they possess? Then there is the issue of GP recruitment: GPs may not be attracted to nurse-led pilots if they fear that becoming accountable to a nurse will inhibit their clinical freedom. Finally, there is the recruitment of the rest of the team, including other clinicians, managers and administrative staff. It is essential to ensure that all staff are signed up to the core values and beliefs of the new model of service.

Nurse-led sites must also manage performance. For nurses to feel confident in new roles they must have appropriate levels of clinical supervision and long-term training. The nurse-led pilots are developing a shared network for learning and development, including the use of telephone and video conferencing to provide training, peer support and clinical supervision. In Warrington there is a system of clinical supervision in place within the Trust that will be extended to the pilot.

Acceptance of nurse-led practices

Nurse-led practices may present a threat to GPs who feel that their power base is being eroded. However, nurse-led pilots offer a new approach to care and do not negate the need for a GP. Gardner[19] describes the care approach provided by nurse-led sites as 'empowering, enabling and educating' patients. In areas where nurse-led pilots are in place, the GPs attached to the sites firmly believe that nurse-led pilots enable the GP to provide improved levels of care to patients.[20] In a study of the Salford nurse-led pilot, Chapple and Sergison[21] found that practice staff felt very anxious at the start of the project but that this quickly changed to enthusiasm.

Prior to the establishment of the nurse-led pilots it was feared that patients might feel that they would receive a second-rate service from a nurse-led pilot. Within the Salford pilot there has been a 12 per cent increase[22] in the practice list size since the pilot commenced. The southern Derbyshire pilot is experiencing steady growth in its list size, with 1000 new patients registering over the first ten months.[23] Patients do not appear to have found the new model off-putting. Chapple and Macdonald[24] found that 'almost all [the patients] who were interviewed spoke enthusiastically and positively about the care that they had received since the nurse-led service started ...'.

Conclusion

The development of nurse-led PMS pilots is a major move forward for the nursing profession as it gives nurses an opportunity to take a more active role in developing future services. It gives nurses the recognition they have long sought by placing an emphasis on the particular skills they bring to primary care. The key question to be addressed during the life of these pilots is whether they present a cost-effective model for primary care delivery.

In the independent contractor and community trust models of nurse-led PMS pilots, the question remains as to the ability of nurses to manage the clinical workload without onward referral to a GP. Within the 'nurse as equal partner' model it will be important to evaluate how appropriately patients select the professional for first contact.

PMS pilots present an opportunity to explore a range of models, not to replace GP-led primary care. In areas that have problems recruiting and retaining GPs, the nurse-led option may provide an appropriate alternative. This is particularly relevant to inner cities with relatively large deprived and homeless populations – communities that nurse practitioners have in the past provided services to.[25, 26]

The NHS is organisationally geared to the traditional model
practice, as shown by the many challenges faced by nurse-led sit‹
of prescribing, administration, registration and information systems.
This compromises the ability of the nurse pilots to test out new models.

A mixed market is developing among the nurse-led sites which mirrors
the diversity within general practice. The nurse-led pilots should offer
many insights into the feasibility of new models of delivering primary
care services. These will be invaluable to the PCGs and PCTs that will be
responsible for the configuration of primary care in the future.

References

1. Royal College of Nursing. *Standards for nursing practice*. London: Scutari, 1911.
2. Hasler J. The primary health care team: history and contractual farces. *British Medical Journal* 1992; 305: 232–34.
3. Rowley E. The role of the practice nurse. In: Hunt G and Wainwright P. *Expanding the role of the nurse: the scope of professional practice*. London: Blackwell, 1994.
4. Hasler J. The primary health care team: history and contractual farces. *British Medical Journal* 1992; 305: 232–34.
5. Higgins P. The nursing profession – a changing role in a changing world. *Journal of the Royal Society of Health* 1996: 51–56.
6. Rowley E. The role of the practice nurse. In: Hunt G and Wainwright P. *Expanding the role of the nurse: the scope of professional practice*. London: Blackwell, 1994.
7. Stillwell B. Developing experts: the nurse in general practice. In: Littlewood J, editor. *Current issues in community nursing: primary healthcare in practice*. London: Churchill-Livingstone, 1995: 128.
8. Chambers N. *Nurse practitioners in primary care*. Abingdon: Radcliffe Medical Press, 1998.
9. Trnobranski PH. Nurse practitioner: redefining the role of the community nurse? *Journal of Advanced Nursing* 1994; 19: 134–39.
10. Chambers N. *Nurse practitioners in primary care*. Abingdon: Radcliffe Medical Press, 1998.
11. Royal College of Nursing. *Nurse practitioner in primary health care – role definition*. London: RCN, 1989.
12. Lenehan C. Nurse practitioners in primary care: here to stay? *British Journal of General Practice* 1994: 291–92.

13. National Health Service Executive. *Nurse prescribing: implementing the scheme across England.* (HSC 1998/232). London: National Health Service, 1998.

14. Department of Health. *Primary Care: The Future – choice and opportunity.* London: HMSO, 1996.

15. Department of Health. *Primary Care: delivering the future.* London: HMSO, 1996.

16. Agrew T. Sheffield nurses lead the field with bid to employ GP. *Nursing Times* 1997; 93(28): 9.

17. Gardner L. Nurse-led Primary Care Act Pilot schemes: threat or opportunity? *Nursing Times* 1998; 94(27): 52–53.

18. Schofield J. Pilot light. *Nursing Times* 1999; 95(2): 32–33.

19. Gardner L. Does nurse-led care mean second class care? *Nursing Times* 1998; 94(36): 50–51.

20. Zammit-Maempel J. GP's praise for new nurse-led practice. *Pulse* 16 January 1999: 29.

21. Chapple A and Sergison M. Challenging tradition. *Nursing Times* 1999; 95(12): 32–33.

22. Gardner L, 1998 (personal communication).

23. Baraniak C, 1999 (personal communication).

24. Chapple A and Macdonald W. A nurse-led pilot scheme: the patients' perspective. *Primary Health Care* 1999; 9(4): 16–17.

25. Chambers N. *Nurse practitioners in primary care.* Abingdon: Radcliffe Medical Press, 1998.

26. Lenehan C. Nurse practitioners in primary care: here to stay? *British Journal of General Practice* 1994: 291–92.

Chapter 6

Piloting new employment opportunities for GPs[1]

Toby Gosden, Alison Holbourn, Tim Crossley and Stephen Gillam

KEY POINTS

- While independent contractor status has been popular with most GPs, a common national contract has not been sufficiently flexible to meet the changing needs of GPs. Therefore, an increasing number of GPs are interested in salaried employment as an alternative

- A variety of salaried GP schemes have been in existence for many years but some have lacked sufficient funding and the status of GP principalships

- Salaried GP posts set up within PMS pilots have the flexibility and funding to provide an alternative to independent contractor status

- Issues that have arisen in setting up these posts include overcoming local opposition and designing an attractive employment package that offers a secure income and professional support

- PMS salaried posts may play a significant role in PCGs if they are successful in recruiting and retaining GPs while providing value for money

Introduction

The NHS (Primary Care) Act 1997[2] is perhaps the most significant reform of general medical practice since 1948. The Act creates new options for GPs as the salaried employees of practices or trusts. These new contractual arrangements are being tested within Personal Medical Services (PMS) pilots on a voluntary basis. Some of the policy aims of PMS pilots are to improve the recruitment and retention of GPs and the quality of care in general practice. However, they have the potential to change the nature of general practice more radically.

In this Chapter we briefly describe how the employment status of GPs has evolved in order to understand why salaried employment is being sought as an alternative to the independent contractor model. We contrast the nature of salaried GP schemes in existence prior to the 1997 Act with those offered by PMS pilots. Finally, we discuss the issues that have been encountered in setting up salaried GP principal posts within two PMS sites and what role salaried employment might have in the future.

Background

Since the creation of a National Health Service (NHS) in 1948, GPs have vigorously defended their independent contractor status.[3] Although their hospital colleagues have always been salaried, GPs rejected the option of salaried employment in both the 1965 and 1990 reforms. Independent contractor status has been popular since it gives the GP, amongst other things, financial independence and clinical autonomy. However, over the last 15 years these advantages have been eroded (see Chapter 2). If general practice can be likened to a network of franchises (practices operating under the NHS brand name), then we can see that as they have grown larger government has attempted to regulate the behaviour of the franchisees more.[4] For example, the Conservative Government introduced a new contract for GPs in 1990.[5] One purpose of the new contract was to reduce variations in the quality of general medical care.[6] This was to be achieved by increasing the proportion of GP income derived from capitation payments, changing remuneration for some services from fees to target payments, and introducing new fees for other types of care.

The 1990 contract was successful in increasing the volume of *some* items of care provided in general practice,[7] but it is not clear whether the quality of primary care increased.[8,9] However, it has been argued that the resulting increase in bureaucracy and the increase in hours of availability may have raised stress levels and lowered the morale of the profession. Whilst it is not clear what the impact of the 1990 reforms has been on recruitment and retention in general practice, it is more certain that it did result in changes in the structure of the general practice employment market.[10] The contract has not been sufficiently flexible to accommodate the changing needs of new recruits to general practice. The life-long financial commitment required by the traditional partnership model of general practice may not suit GPs with young families who prefer more flexible working hours. Young GPs may also prefer being able to change practices without the legal wrangles associated with partnership splits.

Early experience of the new 1990 contract, in particular some of the financial incentives, has highlighted the rigidities of the independent contractor model. Specifically, the 1990 contract does not link incentives to the demand for health care and, therefore, does not provide compensation to GPs with high workloads. For example, capitation payments encourage GPs to have large list sizes, but in deprived areas, with high morbidity and demand for care, this often means a demoralisingly high workload. Where practices attempt to reduce this workload to manageable levels by reducing their list size, they are unable to generate sufficient revenue to maintain adequate standards of premises and staffing levels or personal income. Deprivation payments were made to GPs in an attempt to address this deficiency. However, the Jarman index, upon which the level of payment is set, has been heavily criticised and the level of compensation is regarded as inadequate.[11] Both scenarios make it difficult to recruit GPs to these areas and exacerbate the inequitable distribution of GPs.[12]

Much has been written about the increase in levels of stress experienced by GPs as a result of the increase in paperwork and administration required by the 1990 contract.[13,14,15] It has been argued that this has led to difficulties in GP recruitment and retention; however, this evidence is largely anecdotal and more reliable evidence shows no association.[16]

Salaried GP employment: evolution or revolution

While there has always been a minority of GPs in favour of salaried employment,[17,18] this option has become more popular since the reforms of the early 1990s. In 1992, the GMSC carried out a ballot and found that 10 per cent of GPs thought that there should be a salaried service for all GPs, but 55 per cent believed that there should be the option of being salaried for GPs.[19] However, there have always been a number of salaried employment options available for GPs.

GPs in academic departments and in locum, retainer and assistant posts have always received salary-type payments. However, these posts have not offered suitable employment alternatives to those seeking flexible posts. These mainly part-time posts were considered to be remunerated at a level that was proportionately lower than intended average net remuneration for GP principals.[20,21] The GP retainer scheme's format of a maximum of two sessions per week has not been sufficiently flexible for many GPs.[22] GP assistant posts may also have been perceived as being of 'lower status' when compared to GP principals, as well as lacking job security.[23]

Limited provision for the employment of salaried GPs, at the discretion of the Secretary of State, exists under section 56 of the NHS Act 1977. This has been used in a number of cases to provide primary medical services for homeless people. Non-principals number approximately 7000 in England and Wales,[24,25] which implies that nearly 20 per cent of all GP consultations are with GPs receiving a salary-type payment.

The Tomlinson report[26] highlighted the plight of general practice in London and led to the setting up of the London Initiative Zone (LIZ) project.[27] Within LIZ, the workforce flexibilities programme used, amongst other mechanisms, salaried GP posts to enable existing GPs to undertake educational courses to refresh their skills. While this initiative was confined to London, other schemes emerged across the country.[28] In the 'Parachute doctors scheme' in Liverpool and 'Career Start' in Durham, GPs who had recently completed their vocational training were employed in underserved areas to provide much needed skills and services.

At the same time as the PMS pilot initiative was launched, the Government announced that paragraph 52 of the Red Book was being amended to allow GP principals to be employed by other GPs.[29] The cost of employing GPs in these posts was to be reimbursed from within the cash-limited GMS remuneration pool in the same way as other costs are recouped, such as when practice nurses are employed. Additional funds were distributed to health authorities to pump-prime the initiative.

These posts were to achieve specific objectives, for example improving quality and access to care for patient sub-groups such as the homeless. However, it appears that inadequate funding has prevented this scheme's success.[30]

Salaried posts within PMS pilot sites

One of the purposes of the PMS initiative was to improve quality and the recruitment and retention of GPs in deprived areas, thereby addressing health inequalities. These pilots have the opportunity to create well-funded, salaried posts that will offer a serious alternative employment option to independent contractor status for those GPs who seek greater flexibility.

The NHS (Primary Care) Act 1997 provided the legal framework within which practices, trusts or other bodies within the 'NHS family', could employ GP principals. Over half of the first wave of PMS pilots included one or more salaried GP posts.[31] Salaried GPs are employed by acute or community trusts, single or multiple practices and nurses. These pilots have two main types of practice-based contract. PMS pilots deliver those services that were previously called general medical services; 'PMS-plus' pilots provide additional specialist hospital or community services. Consequently, salaried GPs may be used to perform the same duties as independent contractor GPs or to deliver care to specific patient sub-groups, such as the homeless or drug misusers. There are three main types of salaried GP posts within these pilots:

- GPs who remain in their practice but change their employment status
- GPs who are employed to fill existing GP vacancies
- new posts where the salaried GP is employed in addition to the existing medical workforce.

To illustrate the issues involved in the setting up and operation of salaried GP posts in PMS sites we have chosen two pilot sites which have all three types of post.

Case study 1: Wolverhampton

Objectives

A PMS pilot site in Wolverhampton aims to improve recruitment and retention by employing three single-handed GPs in a deprived inner city area where existing GPs have high list sizes. The pilot recognises that GP registrars are increasingly reluctant to 'become businessmen and women', and that some GPs perceive the disadvantages of being self-employed, such as capital investment, as greater than the advantages, arguably in taxation and clinical autonomy. Two of the salaried posts are held by existing GPs who switched to salaried status; the third post was a new practice starting from scratch. The local community trust employs the GPs and is responsible for the management of their practices with a local independent contractor GP, who is the clinical director for the pilot. As a result of this arrangement the pilot has reduced the non-clinical administrative duties of GPs, enabling them to focus more on clinical work. It has also gained some economies of scale by subsuming the management of all three practices within the trust's infrastructure.

Case study 2: Warrington

Objectives

The second case study has a very different objective. Historically, GPs have been employers and very much leaders of the primary health care team. This PMS-plus pilot has taken a fresh approach in using the salaried option to achieve three inter-related objectives:

- to break down barriers between staff groups and create an integrated primary care team
- to encourage multidisciplinary accountability for the delivery of defined clinical outcomes
- to ensure that patients have access to the most appropriate skills to meet their needs.

Under the 1990 contract, GPs are individually responsible for providing services linked to fees and target payments. However, this pilot has a practice-based contract specifying clinical standards which all primary care team members are responsible for delivering. To encourage this multidisciplinary approach further, different professional groups have equal voting rights on a local management board. The salaried GP has the same status as the rest of the primary care team, which he regards as an advantage since it provides 'the opportunity to work with other professionals of similar enthusiasm and vision'.

The PMS-plus practice contract is tailored to meet specific local health needs. This framework has allowed the salaried GP to extend his interests in the delivery of primary health care beyond the scope possible under the constraints of the Red Book.

Setting up the posts

The success of PMS pilots in recruiting and retaining salaried GPs in posts that would not otherwise be filled could depend on the 'employment package'. GPs who apply for salaried posts may be a particular group, with special needs and specific expectations of salaried status. Young GPs may not want to commit themselves to a particular area or to a long-term partnership. GPs with young families may prefer part-time contracts with flexible working hours.

There are also those GPs who currently work in deprived areas who would like higher salaries than would be possible under the Red Book in order to compensate for poorer working conditions. Therefore, deciding on the levels of contractual benefits, such as salary and fixed hours, and whether the contract includes out-of-hours responsibilities and protected time for professional development, is crucial.

The Warrington pilot employment package attracted some 46 requests for the information pack. The enquiries for the Warrington post highlighted such concerns about salaried status as the protection of pension arrangements and clinical autonomy. Twelve high quality applications were received, and six of these were shortlisted for interview. Most of the applicants for the post were GP principals in NHS general practice. Interviewees for the post expected salaried status to offer freedom from items of service administration and business management concerns, and professional development opportunities.

The Wolverhampton pilot employment package has proved attractive for the two GPs who were already in their posts. In trying to recruit a GP to the newly created post the pilot found that whilst the package interested new doctors it did not get many applications from existing single-handed GPs. This may be largely to do with the fear of losing clinical autonomy. The pilot had nine applicants, shortlisted six and felt five were appointable at interview.

Professional opposition

As additional GPs are recruited into deprived areas, the list sizes of incumbent GPs may be reduced, thereby affecting their income. Thus, salaried GPs may face opposition from neighbouring GPs. Salaried GPs may also encounter difficulties in joining some GP co-operatives, which require that members hold lists.

In Wolverhampton, the local medical committee (LMC) took a neutral stance overall. They supported the idea of increasing the number of doctors but had particular concerns about the likely success of the pilot's management and the pensions arrangements for the employed GPs. In reality, some doctors faced a reduction in pension rights whilst others benefited. The Wolverhampton pilot sought independent advice for all doctors proposing to join them; as a result of this, one doctor was advised not to become salaried whilst others were reassured.

The Warrington pilot was initially supported by the LMC and no major formal opposition was encountered, although several GPs considered the proposal controversial. In part, the project was not opposed because it set out to serve a new housing development in a green field site. It was therefore not directly threatening to any existing practices, and was relieving pressure on an over-stretched system.

Opposition to two other proposed second wave pilots in the town was more pronounced. The opposition focused on the perceived threat of patient migration, but there were also concerns about the intended role and status of nurses and non-medical professionals.

Designing the right contract

The design of the 'right' contract of employment and systems of management will depend upon the role and type of salaried GP. For those GPs who are already in place and simply change their employment status, the 'package' may reflect their current position and salary. However, for pilots hoping to attract GPs to fill a new post or an existing vacancy, setting the salary level, working out pension arrangements and designing management and professional training systems are potentially complex.

The Warrington pilot had to design their model of employment from scratch. There had to be clarity on the trusts' terms and conditions, grievance and disciplinary policies and procedures, the accountability framework, and the clinical support systems in the contract. Paradoxically, PMS sites with a free hand to design contracts wanted guidance. In the absence of this they used as a framework existing trust models of employment or others that are available.[32]

The core elements of the salaried contracts of both pilot sites are shown in Box 6.1:

BOX 6.1: MAIN FEATURES OF THE SALARIED CONTRACTS IN TWO
PMS PILOTS

Element of contract	Warrington	Wolverhampton
Type of employer	Community trust	Community trust
Salary*	£48–58,000	£43,750
Seniority payments?	No	Yes
Hours	37.5	Full-time
Expected to do out-of-hours work?	Yes – GP co-operative	No
Annual leave	30 days + statutory days and bank holidays	25 days + statutory days and bank holidays
Study leave	Yes**	60 hours per year
Private work allowed?	Yes	Yes
Length of contract	Permanent	3 years
Performance related pay?	Partial	N/S***
NHS pension offered/eligible?	Yes	Yes

Notes
* At 1998/99 levels.
** Personal development plans form part of the contract for services with the health authority.
*** N/S – not stated within contract of employment.

Salary and contractual benefits

Both pilot sites used the NHS consultant salary scales as a baseline for
setting the salary levels for the GP posts. The Warrington pilot
recognised that, as they wished to attract a relatively senior GP they

would need to match the likely existing drawings of such a GP. The Wolverhampton salary is based around a list of 1800, and there have been minor adjustments for larger lists. The 'new' practice doctor started at 80 per cent of the above salary, rising to the 100 per cent of the baseline consultant salary over three years. Both salaries compare favourably with the 1998 intended average net remuneration of £47,540 (the notional national income for GPs).

Contractual benefits such as holiday entitlement, sick and maternity leave were determined using Whitley Council conditions as a baseline. The Warrington and Wolverhampton sites offered NHS superannuation scheme membership based on employers' contributions of 8 per cent and employee's contributions of 6 per cent. The disadvantages for GPs of transferring to this pension scheme have been addressed centrally by the Department of Health. For the period of the pilot GPs will be compensated for differences between the levels of their salary-related NHS superannuation and their previous superannuable gross income.

Hours of work and overtime

Salaried employment pays a fixed income to GPs for working a specified number of hours. Unlike the 1990 contract, salaried contracts may also have to specify extra remuneration for GPs who work additional hours.

In the Warrington pilot the salaried GP is contracted to work 37 hours per week but is also a member of the local management board and is therefore expected occasionally to work additional hours within the salary. In the Wolverhampton pilot, hours are defined in a job plan similar to that given to NHS consultants.

Private work

Neither salaried contract restricts the GP from undertaking private work, but both have a clause which requires that any outside working does not impinge on their ability to perform their duties. Independent contractor GPs are contracted to provide a minimum number of hours for patient care and therefore there are few restrictions, in theory, to the amount of time they spend carrying out private work. Salaried GPs, however, will be contracted to provide a set number of hours, both in delivering care and in administrative duties. This is likely to restrict their opportunities to earn income outside of their salaried contract.

Performance related pay, monitoring and accountability

Moving away from the 1990 contract, with its emphasis on the 'quantity' of care, provides pilot sites with the opportunity to set locally determined objectives targeted at improving quality of care. Salaried contracts within the NHS have not historically incorporated explicit performance related pay in the same way as the 1990 contract. Indeed, this may be some of the attraction for GPs of becoming salaried. However, PMS pilots will need to deliver on their objectives and therefore incentive structures might well be designed to ensure this. There is the flexibility within the PMS initiative to experiment with both financial and non-financial incentives. Indeed, the Warrington salaried contract initially contained a performance related pay element but this was subsequently amended. Currently, the salaries of all staff (clinical and non-clinical) are subject to an annual review by the Project Management Board based on:

1. guidance from professional review bodies
2. NHS inflation award.

This arrangement offered the pilot the best framework for keeping pace with national developments on pay and allowing a system that can equally apply to clinicians and non-clinicians. The system recognises the importance to the pilot of a multidisciplinary focus and equity of status and opportunity.

Staff may receive an additional pay uplift if the Project Board feels that they have expanded their role, or performed exceptionally against the contractually agreed criteria within the service agreement. Each staff member is accountable through a clause in their contract of employment for meeting the service objectives of the pilot.

Salaried payment systems are associated with greater levels of management and monitoring of the employee.[33] Therefore, the transition from self-employed GP to salaried employee may require sensitive handling. The success of a salaried scheme for recently qualified GPs in the north west of England has been due to the support and involvement of the GPs in service development.[34] The GPs were given a communication channel for feedback if the management process became unsatisfactory.

In the Warrington pilot, the team (including the GP) reports monthly to the multidisciplinary Project Management Board (see Box 6.2) on the achievement of contractual and organisational objectives. This approach was designed to build positive relationships between all stakeholder organisations and to ensure the right communication channels. In the two second wave pilots proposed in Warrington, in addition to the board members in Box 6.2, there are two user representatives with equal voting rights.

BOX 6.2: WARRINGTON PROJECT BOARD MEMBERS

Project manager

Health Authority Director of Primary Care

Warrington Community Trust Chief Executive

Warrington Community Trust Director of Operations

Local Authority Planning Director

Local Authority Education Officer

Pharmacist

PMS clinicians

Local evaluation representative

The key to setting any performance objectives (whether tied to financial or other incentives or not) is ensuring that they are based on mutually agreed and achievable criteria. Ideally these objectives should relate to evidence of improvements in quality; however, such outcomes are difficult to predict and influence. Therefore, contracts might alternatively focus on 'process measures' of quality such as consultation length.[35]

Training and professional development

Part of the appeal for GPs of becoming an employee is the opportunity to have dedicated time to develop clinical skills and further specialist interests. The 1990 contract provided the incentive to undertake training through the postgraduate education allowance (PGEA), but salaried contracts may be more effective in ensuring that GPs have regular protected training opportunities. Where trusts employ GPs more resources may be available to undertake this professional development. The Warrington post has funds that will finance the continuation of a diploma in therapeutics leading to a Masters degree. Other opportunities for development might include study leave, funded postgraduate education, or a mentor to oversee the professional development and training of the salaried GP.

Conclusion – the future

If the salaried GP posts within PMS pilots are successful in improving recruitment, retention and quality of care, then salaried employment for GPs may become widespread. Improvements in recruitment and retention will depend on whether the GPs' expectations of salaried status are met. PMS salaried GP posts may also have implications for access to care in so far as such schemes tackle GP recruitment and retention in deprived areas. Increasing the number of GPs in underserved areas may go some way towards addressing health inequalities. Salaried employment may overcome some of the rigidities associated with the 1990 contract but will not ameliorate all the barriers to recruitment in these areas. For example, some of the disincentives to working in deprived areas, such as threats to personal safety and excessive workloads, may still remain.

A crucial factor in determining success is whether the pilots overcome some of the difficulties encountered by the previous salaried schemes, such as status and funding. The status of the salaried GP within PMS pilot practices is likely to vary, depending on the type of employer, level of remuneration, and management and accountability arrangements. Even if these schemes do prove more successful in recruiting and retaining GPs and increasing the quality of care, any increases in costs may raise doubts as to whether they are value for money.

Funding for PMS pilots is often based on historical payments and, therefore, it is unclear whether salaried employment will raise costs or produce savings. It is difficult to determine whether a salaried GP 'costs' more than an independent contractor GP since they have different responsibilities. Potential drivers of cost include higher employer's National Insurance contributions and cover for sickness and out-of-hours work.

In addition, many GPs are looking to salaried employment to remove the burden of their administration and management duties. This may increase costs if extra management support needs to be procured. The inclusion of previously uncosted time for professional development activities adds to these pressures.

The future of salaried posts may thus be determined by the availability of additional funds to finance these costs, especially in inner cities where the PMS budget might be low if it is based on historical GMS income. One source of additional funds is the national GP remuneration 'pool'. However, to redistribute this in order to ensure a more equitable distribution of resources may be politically unacceptable. Funding might also come from savings made within the pilot as a result of a reduction in the bureaucracy associated with the 1990 contract.

PMS salaried schemes may have far reaching consequences for the general medical profession. Professional bodies such as the BMA are anxious to protect the independent contractor status for GPs. If PMS salaried GP posts are successful then widespread growth of these and existing non-principal posts could weaken the political muscle of general practice.

The future of salaried contracts for GPs may be largely determined by their potential role in primary care groups and trusts.[36] PCGs have to deliver Health Improvement Programme objectives. Salaried contracts for GPs could help them to do this by tackling recruitment and retention and quality of care issues in their areas. Therefore, the progress of PMS pilots in tackling these issues and providing value for money will be watched closely by PCG chief executives. The danger is, however, that using the salaried status to control GP behaviour may have consequences for GP morale and, therefore, recruitment and retention.

References

1. The authors would like to thank Dr C-K Khomg, Warrington for his help in writing this Chapter.
2. NHS Executive. *Personal Medical Services pilots under the NHS (Primary Care) Act 1997. A comprehensive guide.* London: HMSO, 1997.
3. Lewis J. *Independent Contractors: GPs and the GP Contract in the Post-War Period.* University of Manchester: National Primary Care Research and Development Centre, 1997.

4. Iliffe S. Thinking through a salaried service for general practice. *British Medical Journal* 1992; 304: 1456–57.

5. Department of Health. *General practice in the NHS. A new contract.* London: HMSO, 1989.

6. *Variations between general practitioners.* OHE Briefing No. 26. July 1990.

7. Lynch ML. The uptake of childhood immunisation and financial incentives to general practitioners. *Health Economics* 1994; 3: 117–25.

8. Lowy A, Brazier J, Fall M, Thomas K, Jones N, Williams B. Quality of minor surgery by general practitioners in 1990 and 1991. *British Journal of General Practice* 1994; 44: 364–65.

9. Scott A and Maynard A. *Will the new GP contract lead to cost effective medical practice?* University of York: Centre for Health Economics Discussion Paper 82, 1991.

10. Young R and Leese B. *Recruitment and retention of general practitioners: a review of the UK literature.* University of Manchester: National Primary Care Research and Development Centre, 1998.

11. Carlisle R, Johnstone S and Pearson J. Relation between night visit rates and deprivation measures in one general practice. *British Medical Journal* 1993; 306: 1383–85.

12. Gravelle H and Sutton M. Trends in the geographical equity in GP provision in England and Wales. *The Lancet* 12 December 1998: 1910.

13. Hayter P, Peckham S and Robinson R. *Morale in general practice.* Southampton: Institute for Health Policy, University of Southampton, 1996.

14. Myerson S. The effects of policy change on family doctors. *Journal of Management in Medicine* 1993; 7(2): 7–26.

15. Hannay D, Usherwood T and Platts M. Workload of general practitioners before and after the new contract. *British Medical Journal* 1992; 304: 815–18.

16. Lambert T, Goldacre MJ, Parkhouse J, Edwards C. Career destinations in 1994 of United Kingdom graduates of 1983: results of a questionnaire survey. *British Medical Journal* 1996; 312: 893–97.

17. The British Institute of Public Opinion. The White Paper and the Questionary. *British Medical Journal Supplement* 1944: 25.

18. PRO, MH 153/275, General Practice Working Party (Fraser working Party), Evidence from General Practitioners Association.

19. *Electoral Reform Ballot Services. Your choices for the future: a survey of GP opinion.* London: General Medical Services Committee, 1992.

20. Osler K. Employment experiences of vocationally trained doctors. *British Medical Journal* 1991; 303: 762–64.

21. Douglas A and McCann I. Doctor's retainer schemes in Scotland: time for change? *British Medical Journal* 1996; 313: 792–94.

22. Harrison J and Van Zwanenberg T, editors. *GP Tomorrows.* Oxford: Radcliffe Press, 1998.

23. Allen I. *Part-time working in general practice.* London: Policy Studies Institute, 1992.

24. Sykes M. *Recent local and national trends in GP workforce.* Unpublished survey.

25. Muller E. Survey of doctors who work as non-principals in general practice in Staffordshire. *West Midlands Journal of Primary Care* 1997; 1: 66–71.

26. Department of Health. *Report of the Inquiry into London's Health Service, Medical Education & Research.* HMSO: London, 1992 (The Tomlinson Report).

27. Department of Health. *Making London better.* London: Department of Health, 1993.

28. Harrison J and Van Zwanenberg T, editors. *GP Tomorrows.* Oxford: Radcliffe Press, 1998.

29. NHS Executive. *Salaried Doctor's Scheme.* Leeds: Department of Health FHSL, 1997: 46.

30. Anon. Ministers step in to save salaried posts. *GP* 4 June 1999.

31. Lewis R, Jenkins C, Gillam S. *Personal Medical Services pilots in London. Rewriting the Red Book.* London: King's Fund Publishing, 1999.

32. The Medical Practitioner's Union. *Salaried Service: Threat or Opportunity? Practice guidelines from the MPU.* London: MSF, 1997.

33. O'Connor S and Lanning J. The end of autonomy? Reflections on the postprofessional physician. *Health Care Management Review* 1992; 17(1): 63–72.

34. Woodward R and Shridhar S. Drawing young blood. *Health Service Journal* 1997; 107: 28–29.

35. Howie J. Porter A, Heaney D, Hopton J. Long to short consultation ratio: a proxy measure of quality of care for general practice. *British Journal of General Practice* 1991; 41: 48–54.

36. Health Service Circular. *The New NHS. Modern and Dependable. Developing Primary Care Groups.* London: NHSE, 1998.

Chapter 7

Contracting for primary care

Rod Sheaff

KEY POINTS

- PMS contracts have the potential to involve GPs in implementing national health policy objectives and improve the management of primary care

- Techniques for writing and using PMS contracts for these purposes remain underdeveloped

- In first wave PMS contracts, service objectives were usually stated in broad, non-specific terms

- First wave PMS contract incentives differed little from those in the 'Red Book' and were seldom related to contract objectives

- Similarly, first wave PMS contract monitoring mechanisms tended to be under-specified and not related to contract objectives

- PCGs and GPs need to develop other means of governance such as the use of informal and professional relationships to supplement the PMS contractual framework

---

Contracts as means of governance

For the foreseeable future, contracts (now renamed 'service agreements') are likely to remain an important means whereby governments, through health authorities (HAs) and primary care groups/trusts (PCGs/PCTs), attempt to manage the way in which GPs, community health services and other PHC providers supply primary health care and implement national health policy. This Chapter outlines the results of recent research into the state of contracting for primary medical care in England.

Since 1947 nearly all English GPs have worked under contract to the NHS (formally, to the Secretary of State for Health). Before the NHS was created, GPs served a mixture of private patients (who paid out-of-pocket or were privately insured) and National Insurance patients. Consequently, GPs received a complex mixture of fees-for-service and, for some insured and National Insurance patients, capitation payments. Although the Beveridge report[1] criticised this complex system, strong signs of it remained when the NHS constructed its nationally uniform GP contract. The general medical services (GMS) contract pays GPs through a still complicated and fragmented mixture of capitation and 'item of service' payments which the Red Book sets out in close detail.

The GMS contract was updated in 1990, for example by adding target payments for health promotion work and (subsequently) promoting more organised provision of out-of-hours cover. GP fundholding involved the introduction of prescribing budgets (and indicative prescribing budgets for non-fundholders) and an expansion of practice-based services, further complicating the financial organisation of general practice. Nevertheless, by the mid 1990s it was evident that the GMS contract was becoming unsuited to NHS conditions in several ways:

1. standard payments provided no direct means for increasing payments to attract GPs into relatively unattractive, underserved areas – especially the centres and poorer suburban areas of large cities
2. the GMS contract did not provide any easy means of paying GPs to concentrate on specific care groups
3. GPs were paid for their number of listed patients and for specific activities, not for raising the clinical quality of care or improving other aspects of patients' experience of NHS primary care. However, variations in GP prescribing and referral rates were *prima facie* evidence of an uneven quality of care in NHS general practice. Unsafe practice was dealt with through professional discipline (GMC procedures) and the civil law
4. the GMS system allowed few direct incentives for GPs to change the ways they provided primary care in response to accelerating changes in the hospital sector (shorter lengths of stay, earlier discharge, greater use of day surgery, and so on)
5. under the GMS contract GPs receive both the capitation and item-of-service payments, mainly for treating their listed patients.

This essentially residence-based system is not well adapted to reward treatment of more mobile, marginal populations such as homeless people, students and refugees

6. contracts for GPs and their practice-based services were separated from contracts for community health services. Whatever co-ordination that occurred did so despite, not because of, the contracting process
7. administration of the GMS contracts was routinised, fragmented and complex. The resulting data collection focused on the volume of GP activity and payments. Even these data were under-collected in many practices
8. at practice and at GP level, GMS contracts are not cash-limited in regard to GPs' core medical activity. The cost of general practice thus rose faster than that of the rest of the NHS during the 1990s, despite the Government's policy of minimising the growth of NHS spending
9. the legislation under which the GMS contract was framed also gave independent contractor general practitioner doctors a monopoly in providing primary medical care. This long-standing monopoly contradicted the Conservative Government's policy of weakening professional monopolies in the interests of competition.

The merits of the GMS contract should also be acknowledged. It helped promote the equalisation of GPs' workloads, at least in terms of list sizes. For GPs, national-level bargaining made for consistent expectations and rules, powerful professional bodies and a degree of self-determination at local level. Because of the substantial (latterly, over 50 per cent) capitation element, GPs face a weaker perverse incentive to over-treat patients than, say, NHS dentists do. Since the 1960s, GP doctors have also gravitated towards working in health centres and group practices. The GMS contract's lack of specificity about clinical practice gave space for innovation. Nevertheless, by the late 1990s the GMS contract had become, on balance, an obstacle to levelling up the quality of primary care, increasing its accessibility in urban areas, and to responding to changes in secondary care.

Accordingly the NHS (Primary Care) Act 1997 modified the GMS framework by permitting locally negotiated GP contracts, salaried general practice and other professions to act as lead clinicians in primary care. Personal Medical Service (PMS) contracts should, first, improve the supply of GP services in underserved areas and for other priority care groups (e.g. homeless, students). More generally, PMS contracts are also intended to give HAs a more powerful means of inducing GPs to contribute to implementing HA and government health policy priorities (including Health Improvement Programme priorities). For these purposes, PMS contracts seem intended to promote cost control, incentivisation and managerial accountability in general practice, enabling a shift towards a specification of primary health care based more on evidence-based practice and health outcomes than simple activity. In a move towards integrating primary care, PMS contracts also allow GPs to provide community health services that were formerly provided by NHS trusts (so-called 'PMS-plus' contracts). The contracts further permit HAs to try out new forms of primary care provider organisation. This has led to a few nurse providers taking on the same contractual role as an independent contractor GP (see Chapter 5).

The contract documents are important as evidence of how far PMS contracts are actually changing the governance of primary care, or even threatening GP independence as some critics have alleged (e.g. Reggler, 1998[2]). The aim of the research described in this Chapter was to investigate how far PMS contracts were providing a framework of governance in which GPs functioned as the agent of their health authority and in the implementation of national health policy. The content analysis was intended to reveal what objectives the PMS contracts were stipulating, how precisely, with what incentives for primary health care providers to implement them, and with what arrangements for monitoring the resulting services. A coding frame covering these points was devised, tested for reliability and modified accordingly. Contract documents were collected, their contents coded onto a spreadsheet and then analysed to yield mainly descriptive statistics. The figures below summarise contracts covering 71 PMS pilots (85 per cent of the first wave).

The documents have to be interpreted in the light of other, written agreements or statutory requirements, such as prescribing regulations. Further, documents are one thing and practice is another. Either party may choose not to exercise their contractual rights fully[3] or, conversely, do more than their minimum contractual requirements. For example, only two of the PMS contracts we analysed stipulated monthly financial monitoring, although NHS trust managers usually monitor all budgets every month. Consequently the content analysis was interpreted in the light of interviews with GPs and managers at PMS sites selected to cover the maximum variety of organisational forms.

Organisational forms

Although nearly half of the PMS contracts mentioned new forms of primary care provider, the number of these providers was so small that they remain exceptional. Thirty-one (43 per cent) of first wave contracts were made with nurse-led providers or NHS trusts employing salaried GPs, although 44 contracts (62 per cent) allowed the option for GPs to become salaried (however the fact that the contract permits salaried general practice does not mean that the option has actually been taken up). Nurse-led schemes are rarer still (see Chapter 5). Although current health policy advocates that GPs and HAs collaborate with social services[4, 5] only five sites (7 per cent) stipulated that PMS pilot providers would offer patients advice on how to access social services, and just one contract (1 per cent) explicitly named social services as a co-provider.

PMS-only (as opposed to PMS-plus) contracts leave general practice broadly as it was under GMS without adding or subtracting services. Over two-thirds (69 per cent) of first wave PMS pilot contracts were of this kind. However, PMS contracts can specify such requirements as surgery hours, and 32 contracts (45 per cent) did so. Another 15 (21 per cent) only required that providers should supply whatever hours of service their practice leaflet promised. From the contracts it was impossible to tell whether these hours of service were longer or shorter than before.

Interviews with GPs and managers suggested that the GPs saw PMS contracts as a means to acquire extra services and resources for their practices, either by taking over CHS services, by encouraging GPs to develop specialised clinical interests or by producing economies of scale in management. One site also used the scheme to promote cross-referral between GPs as a way of substituting GP minor surgery for hospital referrals, thereby saving money, which the GPs could re-invest. PMS contracts that allowed salaried practice also enabled GPs to alleviate the organisational problems of small practices (e.g. finding study leave cover) and reduce their burden of administrative work. For HAs, the contracts, as policy-makers intended, did provide a new way of recruiting medical or nursing cover for hard-to-fill vacant practices. However, other aspects of the regulatory framework have not been remodelled, making it needlessly difficult for HAs to recruit new GPs opportunistically to PMS contracts when practices with GMS contracts fall vacant.

Contract objectives

The NHS Executive is evaluating first wave PMS pilots in terms of what they contribute to the realisation of policy objectives of 'quality', 'fairness', 'accessibility', 'responsiveness' and 'efficiency' in primary health care.[6] With regard to PMS contracts, the results are as follows: effective service delivery was mentioned in 52 contracts (73 per cent), good employment practice in 48 (68 per cent), fair access to services in 46 (65 per cent), public involvement in service planning or monitoring in 40 (56 per cent), improving population health in 38 (54 per cent) and improving patient and/or carer experience in 35 (49 per cent). Service efficiency was mentioned as a general objective in 32 cases (45 per cent), PHCT skill-mix changes being stipulated in 30 (42 per cent). The same number of contracts stated an objective of implementing HA strategy. Four contracts (6 per cent) duly required the provider to implement the HA's Health Improvement Programme, although the Programme cannot have been written when the contracts were drafted. National policy objectives tended to be mentioned briefly and in broad terms, rarely as specific operational objectives. For instance, health objectives were seldom translated into outcome indicators. 'Efficiency' was almost always paraphrased as 'value for money' rather than being quantified. As extreme cases, 16 contracts (23 per cent) stated no explicit objectives at all.

Quality

Quality of clinical work is subsumed within the policy of clinical governance and is of particular interest. Contracts specified the quality of primary medical care in various ways. Most stipulated a specific complaints procedure (56 contracts, 79 per cent) and what qualifications the GPs (46 contracts, 65 per cent) and/or other health workers should have (31 contracts, 44 per cent). Standards for premises were defined in 40 (56 per cent) of contracts, although only by appealing to the old GMS rules on that point. Thirty-two contracts (45 per cent) stated that clinical audit should be performed, which was already practically mandatory under the GMS regime. Twenty-two contracts (31 per cent) stated that clinical practice should be evidence-based, although few said what evidence should be applied or how. Eleven contracts (15 per cent) stated that the GPs should follow expert consensus on good practice and just three (4 per cent) required the use of patient-defined outcomes of care. Use of guidelines, protocols and pathways was required in 43 contracts (61 per cent), but particular examples were rarely stipulated. Rather, the contracts required providers to develop their own during the contract term.

Incentives and penalties

Without incentives and ways of monitoring that providers have delivered, contracts run the risk of becoming empty declarations. As payments to providers for realising these objectives, 55 contracts (77 per cent) offered block sums, usually calculated by totalling the previous year's GMS payments and then adjusting at the margin (e.g. to reflect known population changes). PMS contracts all presuppose that the levels and quality of general medical services will be no lower than before. Providers' costs for surgery premises, staff, pharmaceuticals, etc., are likely to have been more or less unchanged in real terms, so the residue which constitutes the GPs' personal incomes will also remain close to its level (real terms) under the GMS contract. In 18 contracts (25 per cent), the block payment excluded the incentive payments for GPs to reach the vaccination and immunisation targets introduced in the 1990 GMS contract, but these contracts offered such target payments as additions and on the same basis as before. Just three contracts (4 per cent) prescribed penalties and two (3 per cent) a bonus, but all these penalties and bonuses were for data provision (i.e. administrative activity) rather than reaching health care or policy objectives.

Just under a quarter (24 per cent) of the PMS contracts anticipated that the provider might make savings on the cost of providing the contracted services. Most (15 contracts, 21 per cent) let the providers keep all these savings, although seven (10 per cent) restricted spending them to purposes that the HA approved, and eight more (11 per cent) restricted spending to the development of patient services. None of the PMS contracts distinguished savings due to initially over-estimating costs and payments from savings resulting from efficiency gains.

During the mid 1990s both the Audit Commission[7] and the national press criticised GP fundholders for spending savings from their budgets for secondary and community services on practice premises. This was because the GP would benefit personally when he or she eventually sold the premises. No PMS contracts forbade this use of savings made in providing primary health services.

Monitoring

As for monitoring services to confirm that they satisfied the contract, 23 contracts (32 per cent) stipulated an annual report on services, 24 contracts (34 per cent) a quarterly report and only two contracts (3 per cent) monthly monitoring. Nearly all of the contracts (96 per cent) arranged for the HA to monitor the PMS contract and services, together with the local community health council in six cases (8 per cent) and 'users' in another four (6 per cent). No contracts used exception reporting, i.e. requiring the providers to report any cases where services were not provided as specified. 15 contracts (21 per cent) required nationally recognised data formats (including a few internationally recognised formats). In practice, though, many providers may have already been supplying monitoring data in standard formats before 1998. About a fifth of the contracts (15, 21 per cent) proposed to compare PMS pilot data with the last year of GMS data. Only three contracts (4 per cent) intended to benchmark against other providers' activity and costs. Most contracts (52, 73 per cent) stipulated a formal evaluation of the PMS pilot but, considering this was a precondition for achieving PMS pilot status, the figure is remarkably low. In general, therefore, PMS pilot contracts required more monitoring data than GMS contracts. Nevertheless, the vague specification of contract objectives, the broad incentives and the nature of monitoring imply that it will be difficult for HAs to collect hard evidence of whether or not the contract objectives have been fulfilled.

Conclusions

PMS contracts are a means to achieve potentially far-reaching changes in the governance and organisational structures of NHS primary care. The evidence cited above indicates that, in general:

1. national health policy objectives figured in most of the contracts, indicating that PMS contracts could serve as a way of involving GPs in implementing these objectives
2. the techniques of writing and using PMS contracts as an instrument of governance are as yet underdeveloped
3. contract objectives were usually stated in very broad, non-specific terms
4. contract incentives differed little from those in the GMS contract. Rarely were they coupled to the contract objectives
5. the contracts under-specified the monitoring mechanisms and those that were specified tended not to focus on the contract objectives.

Although they have considerable scope for development, PMS contracts as they currently exist are of limited use as means for HAs or PCGs to manage general practice. They are of equally limited use, as yet, for integrating general practice with community health services or perhaps, as *Partnership in Action* suggests, social services in the longer term.[8] Whilst work is taking place to refine PMS contracting techniques, HAs and PCGs will need to develop other means of governance alongside stronger information systems, use of informal and professional relationships, and collaboration with professional bodies.

In the meantime, a second wave of PMS pilots began in October 1999. The Health Bill places the 1997 Act's provision for PMS contracts on a permanent footing. PMS contracts will thus remain an important governance option for PCGs and PCTs. The Government has promised that all GPs who wish to remain independent contractors may do so. PCTs are permitted to take over PMS contracts with GPs, enabling them to use PMS contracts as their main medium of governance and management in primary care.[9] Lamentations about the end of GP independence are both premature and beside the point. PMS contracts may conserve GP independence, and they are not inconsistent with independent contractor status. However, they do require GPs to consider actively what services their practices are to provide, why and for whom, and to decide how far and in what capacity they wish to participate in the management of NHS primary care.

References

1. Beveridge W. *Social Insurance and Allied Services*. London: HMSO, 1942.
2. Reggler J. My point-by-point rejection of deal. *Pulse* 27 June 1998: 7.
3. Smith PC. *Devolved Purchasing in Health Care. A Review of the Issues.* London: Nuffield, 1997.
4. Department of Health. *The New NHS – Modern, Dependable*. London: HMSO, 1997.
5. Department of Health. *General Medical Services terms and conditions of service*. London: Department of Health, annual.
6. Department of Health. *Evaluation of Primary Care Act PMS Pilots. Research Brief*. Leeds: Department of Health, 1997 (unpublished).
7. Audit Commission. *Briefing on GP Fundholding*. London: HMSO, 1995.
8. Department of Health. *Partnership in Action*. London: HMSO, 1998.
9. Sheaff R. The development of English Primary Care Group governance. A scenario analysis. *International Journal of Health Planning and Management*. 1999; (4) (forthcoming).

Chapter 8

Information management and technology

Diane Jones

KEY POINTS

- Strategic planning for IM&T is essential for the successful development of PMS pilots

- Different PMS pilots have very different IM&T priorities and no single solution will meet all requirements

- PMS pilots require multidisciplinary involvement in the processes of information management

- PMS pilots are planning innovations in the areas of access to evidence, electronic prescribing and telecare

---

As organisations change, their information requirements also change. The development of new models of health care delivery and new types of organisation through PMS pilots therefore has implications for information management and technology (IM&T).

IM&T development within general practice has been inconsistent. The introduction of the requirement for accreditation (RFA)[1] for GP clinical systems has led to a degree of standardisation, but there are still problems. Some of these stem from poor information technology (IT), but many arise from poor information management and data quality.[2] Although some practices have well developed IT infrastructures with stable information systems and good data quality, many have poor IT systems with poor quality data.

In December 1997, the Government set out its plans to modernise the NHS,[3] and from the outset the use of technology was identified as a key component. Computerised systems and communications technologies are now an intrinsic part of the infrastructure of primary care. Communications technology has already been introduced to primary care, with many practices linked electronically to their health authority to exchange patient and payment information. Some have links with other service providers such as pathology laboratories. The introduction of GP fundholding and total purchasing pilots meant that many practices undertook development of systems to support commissioning.[4]

In 1998, the Prime Minister recognised the 'poor use of IT' in the NHS and the need for the NHS to exploit information resources.[5] He promised to fund developments via the Modernisation Fund. In September 1998, a new information strategy was launched.[6]

In primary care many IM&T developments have focused upon management functions such as financial planning, monitoring budgets, claiming payments, and registering patients. The 1992 information strategy[7] focused upon building an information infrastructure, but has been criticised more recently for giving 'undue priority to management information'.[8] It included many national projects, for example GP/HA links and the implementation of the new NHS number, which had a major impact upon general practice systems. However, there was little overall co-ordination of projects[9] and practices often found themselves inundated with IM&T developments within a very short timescale.

The new strategy, *Information for Health*[10] focuses much more on clinically relevant information systems. One of the key challenges within the strategy is the development of the primary care electronic health record (EHR), which is defined as 'a longitudinal record of patients' health and health care – from cradle to grave'.[11] The importance of high quality information systems with accurate, timely and reliable information is paramount to achieving this objective.

IM&T and PMS

The original guidance from the NHS Executive for first wave PMS pilots provided some general guidance in the use of IM&T resources for PMS pilots. It encouraged pilots to define their information requirements at an early stage but made clear that wholesale replacement or upgrading of practice systems was *not* required or expected.[12] The guidance recommended the use of MIQUEST* to extract data from systems and urged pilots to consider electronic communication.[13] Potential second wave sites received more guidance within the new comprehensive guide,[14] although this remains limited.

In order to develop 'effective solutions and guidance'[15] an evaluation of IM&T in over 20 of the first wave PMS sites was undertaken. However, due to the disparate nature of the PMS pilots it was not possible to draw up a single framework for IM&T development in PMS pilots. Developing IM&T in a PMS site is little different to developing IM&T in any other primary care organisation. However, the PMS pilots are testing new models of working and provide an opportunity to evaluate developments in IM&T in the primary care setting. The rest of this Chapter outlines some of the IM&T issues arising within first wave PMS pilots.

Challenges for first wave PMS sites

Strategic planning

Many PMS pilots have re-evaluated IM&T in order to optimise their resources and plan for future development. The Robert Darbishire Practice in Manchester commissioned an IM&T strategy as a priority for progressing the pilot. The key IM&T priorities for this pilot are included in Box 8.1.

---

* MIQUEST is a software package that allows the trained user to interrogate and extract data from different GP computer systems for the purposes of comparative activity audit and analysis.

Box 8.1: THE ROBERT DARBISHIRE PRACTICE, MANCHESTER

KEY IM&T PRIORITIES

- develop IM&T strategy

- recruit full-time IM&T development manager

- undertake health needs assessment (HNA)

- improve clinical coding to support HNA

- improve communication between primary and secondary care to facilitate 'seamless care' (e.g. by establishing NHS Net connection, implementing email and piloting a national booked admissions project)

- improve access to evidence by via NHS Web

Multi-professional information systems

Among the first wave, over 90 per cent of pilots had computerised age/sex registers and a similar proportion had computerised prescribing information. However, only about 40 per cent of the pilots have complete sets of computerised medical records and five sites were not computerised at all.[16] Some of the PMS pilots are new developments and have therefore been involved in procuring a new system. The Daruzzaman Care Centre in Salford is a new nurse-led pilot whose procurement was complicated by the need to support nurses' information requirements. The clinical systems available are focused upon GP information requirements. The site therefore discussed their specific requirements with the suppliers. One supplier offered to pilot some care planning software already under development, while another offered to work with the lead nurse to develop a new module. The key priorities for developing IM&T at the Daruzzaman Care Centre are included in Box 8.2.

Box 8.2: The Daruzzaman Care Centre, Salford
Key IM&T priorities

- assess information requirements

- develop specification

- evaluate systems

- select system and negotiate development of care plans

- install system and train staff

- establish NHS Net connection

- evaluate use of teleconferencing for peer support and training

- pilot local multidisciplinary evidence centre (LMEC)

Information management

Information management is a key issue, especially for complex multiple practice pilots such as the South West London Primary Care Organisation (SWLPCO). Such pilots must be able to analyse comparative data across all practices. However, as each system is often different and data have been entered in different ways at each site, it is difficult to extract comparative data that are accurate, reliable and consistent. Such pilots need to agree standards for data entry and coding across all sites, irrespective of the actual clinical system being used. This will require decisions being made regarding who should actually enter data, and a training needs assessment followed by appropriate courses for staff. SWLPCO recognised these problems in the early stages of their pilot and made plans to overcome them. Box 8.3 describes the key elements of SWLPCO's IM&T strategy.

BOX 8.3: SOUTH WEST LONDON PRIMARY CARE ORGANISATION
KEY IM&T PRIORITIES

- implement email, NHS Net access and web- and evidence-based medicine at each practice via the Doctor's Desk project

- migrate all practices to the same clinical system

- implement the use of standard primary care data sets and Read codes to enable extraction and comparability of primary care data

- evaluate potential for nurse activity data to be entered onto the GP clinical system

- develop a database to store and analyse primary care data extracted from clinical systems via MIQUEST

Access to evidence

Many PMS sites have defined objectives to improve the quality of care for their patients by developing clinical guidelines. Gaining access to the required literature and critical appraisal skills has proved difficult.

Information for Health stated that all general practices should be connected to the NHS Net by the year 2000[17] and will therefore have access to online resources. This deadline for attaching practices to NHS Net has recently been changed to 2002.[18] However, health professionals also need skills to search the literature, locate documents and critically evaluate material (or have access to someone who has these skills). Although GPs have access to literature via postgraduate libraries, nurses, health visitors and other primary care staff often have limited access to information services. The development of the National Electronic Library for Health (NELH) may improve access to such literature, but it will be some time before NELH is fully functional.

The Warrington Community Trust PMS site is also a pilot for the Local Multidisciplinary Evidence Centre (LMEC) initiative.[19] Within this pilot an information specialist either undertakes literature reviews and obtains documents, or trains staff to undertake their own reviews.

Advice is also given on sources of literature and research methodologies. This enables staff within the PMS pilot to gain access to evidence, and supports their development of guidelines and protocols. Another option may be to consider setting up contracts with local hospital libraries to provide library and information services.

Financial issues

The IT budget within GMS has always been cash-limited and access to funds has often been based on a bidding process. PMS pilots have the opportunity to plan developments over a three-year period on the basis of agreed budgets.

Multi-agency working

Partnerships in Action[20] underlines the importance of shared information across health and social care but highlights shortcomings in information systems – incompatible systems and barriers to sharing information are reasons for lack of progress. Many of the PMS pilots have identified multi-agency working as a key objective, highlighting the need to address these difficulties.

The information required to support integrated care between health and social services must still be determined and *Information for Health* highlights the work required, including agreeing common coding and classification.[21]

Electronic prescribing

Electronic prescribing would involve practices linking their computer to local pharmacies. This would have implications in terms of resources and electronic security but technically it is not difficult to implement. Advantages include the potential audit trail and removal of the need to routinely print prescriptions at the practice. This would reduce paperwork and the risk of stolen prescriptions. Pharmacies could hold information regarding payment exemption and potentially reduce the burden of people not paying for drugs when they should do.

The main barrier to such an electronic link appears to be the Medicines Act 1973,[22] which requires prescriptions to be signed by hand, in ink, by a medical practitioner. An electronic signature is not sufficient. This is particularly pertinent to nurse-led pilots where these legal restrictions are impeding the functioning of the pilot (see Chapter 5).

Telemedicine, telecare and videoconferencing

Telemedicine, telecare and videoconferencing are relatively new within the UK, although projects are being undertaken and evaluated in the NHS, and specifically in primary care.[23] Telemedicine and telecare have already demonstrated potential value in rural areas, where access to secondary care may be difficult.[24] Some of the PMS pilots have already highlighted areas where such technologies could be advantageous. For example, the nurse-led sites are currently assessing the possibility of using videoconferencing to link to each other for training and peer support and to overcome their physical isolation. Potentially, telemedicine could be used in these practices where a GP is not always available onsite.

Conclusion

The PMS pilots provide an opportunity to evaluate IM&T development in a period of organisational change. From the case studies, it is clear that each organisation has different objectives and hence different information and IT 'solutions'. The pilots emphasise the need for strategic planning for IM&T to ensure that organisations have a clear way forward with realistic targets. They underline the importance of information management processes to ensure high quality data.

References

1. NHS Management Executive. *General medical practice computer systems: requirement for accreditation*. Information Management Group, 1993.
2. Jones D. The national information management and technology (IM&T) strategy and its impact upon primary care. Proceedings of the 2nd International Symposium on Health Information Management Research. Sheffield: University of Sheffield, 1996: 53–62.
3. Department of Health. *The New NHS – Modern, Dependable*. London: The Stationery Office, 1997.
4. Leese B and Mahon A. The information requirements of total purchasing projects: implications for primary care groups. *Journal of Management in Medicine* 1999; 13(1): 13–22.

5. The Prime Minister, the Rt. Hon. Tony Blair, speech at the 'All our Tomorrows' Conference. Earl's Court, 2 July 1998 (press notice).

6. NHS Executive. *Information for Health: an information strategy for the modern NHS 1998–2005*. Leeds: NHSE, 1998.

7. NHS Management Executive. *An information management and technology strategy for the NHS in England*. Leeds: NHSME, 1992.

8. NHS Executive. *Information for Health: an information strategy for the modern NHS 1998–2005*. Leeds: NHSE, 1998.

9. National Audit Office. *The 1992 and 1998 information management and technology strategies of the NHS Executive*. London: The Stationery Office, 1999.

10. NHS Executive. *Information for Health: an information strategy for the modern NHS 1998–2005*. Leeds: NHSE, 1998.

11. NHS Executive. *Information for Health: an information strategy for the modern NHS 1998–2005*. Leeds: NHSE, 1998.

12. NHS Executive. *Personal medical services pilots under the NHS (Primary Care) Act 1997: a comprehensive guide*. Leeds: NHSE, 1997.

13. NHS Executive. *Personal medical services pilots under the NHS (Primary Care) Act 1997: a comprehensive guide*. Leeds: NHSE, 1997.

14. NHS Executive. *Personal medical services pilots under the NHS (Primary Care) Act 1997: a comprehensive guide – second edition*. Leeds: NHSE, 1998.

15. NHS Executive. *Personal medical services pilots under the NHS (Primary Care) Act 1997: a comprehensive guide*. Leeds: NHSE, 1997.

16. Leese B, Gosden T, Riley A, Allen L, Campbell S. *Setting Out. Piloting innovations in primary care. Report on behalf of PMS National Evaluation Team*. Manchester: National Primary Care Research and Development Centre, 1999.

17. NHS Executive. *Information for Health: an information strategy for the modern NHS 1998–2005*. Leeds: NHSE, 1998.

18. Department of Health press release 99/476. 'Doctor desktop' computers plan will boost support to GPs. Department of Health: http://www.nds.coi.gov.uk

19. NHS Executive North West R&D Directorate. Local Multidisciplinary Evidence Based Centres: http://www.doh.gov.uk/nwro/lmecinfo.htm 1999

20. Department of Health. *Partnership in action: new opportunities for joint working between health and social services – a discussion document*. London: The Stationery Office, 1998.

21. NHS Executive. *Information for Health: an information strategy for the modern NHS 1998–2005*. Leeds: NHSE, 1998.

22. Medicines Act 1968 (c.67). London: HMSO, 1968.

23. Steele K and Wootton R. Primary care telemedicine in the UK. *British Journal of General Practice* 1997: 4–5.

24. NHS Estates. *Telemedicine. Health Guidance Note*. London: HMSO, 1997.

Chapter 9

Towards primary care organisations – partnership in action?

Tom Butler, Richard Lewis and Ian Ayres

KEY POINTS

- Integrated care is a key policy objective and implies 'whole system' co-ordination and not necessarily the creation of a unified organisation

- There is no single model of integrated care but a number of core elements are identified

- PMS pilots allow a number of organisational, financial and professional barriers to integrated care to be overcome through the creation of primary care organisations

- The Tipton Care Organisation and the South West London Primary Care Organisation developed as first wave pilots and have reduced the level of health service fragmentation

Introduction

PCGs are required to develop primary care, commission hospital and community services, and improve the health of their populations.[1] Co-operation with social care and other organisations will be characteristic of this process. This new partnership approach is intended to inform, plan and implement local Health Improvement Programmes, while retaining the distinction between commissioning and provision of services. PCGs appear to be a transitional form of organisation to primary care trusts (PCTs). Health authorities are responsible for supporting the development of PCGs. Earlier chapters have described the policy background to both these mandatory reforms and the optional PMS initiatives. This Chapter will explore current PMS developments and consider whether they are prototype primary care organisations for the future.

What is integrated health care?

The creation of the NHS was part of a range of public policy initiatives, including income maintenance, education and welfare services. However, each of the elements of this new approach to social policy was rooted in separate organisations. Although health care was popularly seen as a single system, which brought together family doctors and hospital services under the umbrella of the new National Health Service, integrated care remains something distinctly different. There is no single model of integrated care, but the concept has a number of core elements:

- communication that crosses organisational and professional boundaries for individual patients
- clear pathways to gain access to health services
- professional knowledge of the capability and capacity of all forms of health provider
- common standards of professional practice, irrespective of location
- common patient records systems that simultaneously ensure that important information is shared and confidentiality is protected.

Integrated care involves a 'whole systems' approach, i.e. the co-ordination of services rather than the creation of a single organisation to manage organisational relationships, access to services and professional conduct. But what are the barriers to integrated care?

Barriers to integrated primary care

Primary care as practised in Britain since 1948 has been defined as:

> *The provision of first contact and continuing care in the community for patients undifferentiated by age, sex or disease. It is characterised by ease of access to services and provision by generalists health care professionals. It includes general medical, dental, pharmacy, nursing*

and a range of other community services, as well as their relations with informal (family and community) care, hospitals and social care.[2]

However, because of the way in which the welfare state was conceived, organisational, financial and professional barriers were erected between primary, secondary and tertiary health care as well as between health and social care. As a result services were highly fragmented. Regulation was the responsibility of different professional bodies, and budgets could not be shared between services. The regulatory framework created in 1948 has continued to act as a barrier to the development of primary care, and to the implementation of integrated services for professionals and patients alike.[3]

PMS pilots were established to tackle four key policy issues: to reduce variation in the quality of primary care; to remove organisational and financial barriers to improving primary care; to experiment with new models of primary care organisation; and to address local needs by challenging the limitations of the single national GP contract. PMS provided an opportunity, in advance of the emergence of PCGs, to experiment with new models of primary care organisation to address local problems. Is PMS simply an opportunity to work outside the national GMS contract or is it an integral part of the primary care organisation of the future?

Organisational barriers

The separation of general practice, community services, hospital care and social care creates a significant organisational barrier to integrated care. Each organisation has developed separate and distinctive cultures, which reinforce their differences. The introduction of the Community Care Act 1990 provided testimony to these differences. Much of the negotiations between agencies emphasised boundary disputes, rather than collaboration and integration of care planning and delivery. Different agencies defined their area as being in either the 'health' or 'social' care domain.

Financial barriers

Historically the general medical services budget has been separate from the hospital and community health budget. A regulatory framework designed to 'protect' this separation has ensured that neither integrated budgeting nor service delivery has taken place. Originally PMS was to be the vehicle to test the full integration of budgets (GMS non-cash limited, GMS cash-limited, HCHS and prescribing), but the Government stepped back from this more radical stance. PCGs and PCTs have only been bequeathed GMS cash-limited, HCHS and prescribing budgets.

Barriers to quality primary care

The Red Book pays for quantity not quality and assumes GMS to be the same all over the country. In contrast, PMS can reward quality and reflect local need. However, neither PCGs nor PCTs have responsibility for commissioning GMS, although PCTs can commission PMS if local practices are in the scheme. This provides an opportunity to commission care across the primary and secondary sectors (although local development schemes do offer limited opportunities to do this within a GMS framework).

Professional barriers

The NHS has been accused of professional 'tribalism', with competition between different disciplinary groups around 'who does what'. Such approaches can go beyond professional disagreements and become a problem for patients who need access to services from the most appropriate person. One solution to these problems is to experiment with different models of integrated services. This can be done through the substitution of roles and tasks between professionals, for example primary care nurses taking on tasks traditionally done by GPs (see Chapter 5), and GPs developing primary care to do work traditionally confined to the hospital.

How could services be better integrated?

Although PMS sites are in their infancy there are a number of different organisational models emerging to achieve better-integrated services:

- the *leadership model*, in which existing general practices employ salaried staff, including doctors, to work to acknowledged standards of good practice. This approach is intended to improve access to services, especially where GP recruitment has been difficult, and to achieve agreed quality of services
- the *co-operation model*, in which PMS pilots voluntarily agree to co-operate with other organisations such as community trusts to produce agreed policies and practices aimed at the practice population
- the *primary care organisation model* (PCO) is the most radical option as it creates an entirely new organisation to provide integrated primary care. All three models are currently being developed in the PMS pilots.

The distinction between these three models is not absolute, for example a PMS site that began life as a co-operative model could become a PCO. All three models have used the new flexibilities offered by the PMS initiative to find organisational solutions to local service problems.

BOX 9.1: KEY CHARACTERISTICS OF A PRIMARY CARE ORGANISATION

The PCO, in contrast to traditional models of primary care, includes the following features:

- single organisational structure with responsibility for managing *all* primary and community services

- an overarching organisation that forms a relationship with practices grouped into a single body as a federation of practices

- strategic responsibility for health planning, commissioning and delivery, albeit separate from specific general practices.

Such an organisation may have the capacity to deliver the complex agenda on financial, contractual, professional and policy accountability, including quality assurance (as clinical governance), as well as to lead evidence-based service developments. If this arrangement included social care, they would go beyond current proposals for PCTs, pooled budgets and joint commissioning.

PCOs do not necessarily integrate primary and community services, but in the context of PMS-plus, they could take on the employment of community nursing, creating a single organisational structure with responsibility for managing all primary care. This is of course also a function of level 4 PCTs. The flexibility of PMS allows PCOs, larger than traditional practices, to share infrastructure and introduce shared services. PCOs are unlikely to take on strategic responsibility for health planning, commissioning and delivery – they are essentially provider organisations, and will plan delivery within the health planning and commissioning of PCGs/PCTs. They are intrinsically linked to general practice and are essentially ways of sharing the planning and operation of delivering services GMS/PMS and social care within the PCT.

Developing a new primary care organisation

PMS produced a number of new models of primary care and two case studies will be examined here. Further details of these and other sites are provided in the appendix to this book.

Case study 1: The Tipton Care Organisation

Creating a new organisation

This organisation provides primary care services to patients in the Black Country. This is a deprived community of 43,000 patients with 18 GPs from eight practices. The objective of the pilot is to increase access to services, improve quality of services, make more efficient use of resources, and test and demonstrate the benefits of inter-agency working and community involvement. The new organisation will provide 'PMS-plus' services, including the use of salaried general practice. The 'plus' element of the service includes community nursing, midwifery and allied professions as well as the production of integrated packages of clinical and social care. These care packages cover a range of conditions including respiratory disease, diabetes, coronary disease prevention, orthopaedics and pain management. In addition, new services are available through the Citizens Advice Bureau, Family Advice Service, minor illness advice service and rehabilitation care packages.

The plan is to move from a 'virtual' PCO to a 'real' PCO during the life of the project. The virtual organisation is a voluntary alliance of partnership agencies. Six different organisations are currently represented in the virtual PCO: voluntary organisations, the community trust primary care directorate, social services, GPs, patient groups and other health professionals. By encompassing all of these groups within a single organisation, the intention is to achieve greater integration of service planning, management and delivery. An executive group will manage the new organisation and enjoy the benefits of resource sharing through common payroll facilities, formulary, access to repeat prescriptions, better cover to release staff and an integrated programme of continuing professional education.

Accountability in the virtual PCO continues through existing professions and organisations, with shared agreements made by the executive group. When the virtual organisation becomes real, accountability will encompass the whole organisation through the executive, who in turn will be accountable to the commissioning Health Authority (see Figure 9.1).

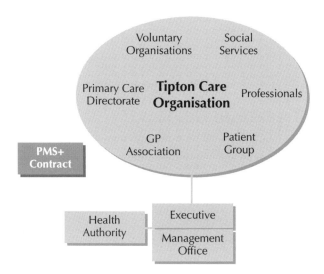

(Adapted from: *Tipton Care Organisation – New Models of Primary Care* pilot summary.)

Figure 9.1: The Tipton Care Organisation

Overcoming fragmentation

It has been argued that one of the defining characteristics of the relationship between health and social care in Britain is fragmentation.[4]

The separation of functions provided through different organisations colours all decision-making. This fragmentation exists *within* organisations between professions and *between* agencies, on boundary disputes around who does what. Creating a new organisation for primary care involves confronting a number of these long-standing problems. The starting point for such an analysis is an assessment of the strengths and weaknesses of traditional health and welfare organisations and a judgement about the potential advantages of a new model over the old. The Tipton example provides a plan for integrated services that creates a single health and social care provider organisation for those who work in and use local services. Methods such as care planning delivery through case management could be used to ensure that a comprehensive view was taken of patient's circumstances and needs. The organisation would have the power to deploy resources across a number of care domains, in contrast to traditional approaches that rely on the distinctions between 'health' and 'social' care. From the user's perspective there are two fundamental changes proposed by the model – users as active partners in the PCO contribute to policy-making and priority setting and, as consumers of the service, they can receive a range of integrated services from a single agency as a 'one-stop shop'.

Case study 2: The South West London Primary Care Organisation

Creating a new organisation

The SWLPCO has formed a single overarching partnership of all 39 GPs for the purpose of providing PMS (see Figure 9.2). One outcome should be improved efficiency – for example, one surgery within the PCO has passed on the responsibility for managing IM&T to the PCO. Other practices are considering this option and similar arrangements are being explored for practice management. The PCO is migrating all its clinical systems to the same supplier and will move to sharing IM&T support and maintenance. As part of the PCG, the PCO is working to develop standardised primary care minimum data sets and clinical code definitions to provide a consistent and effective information platform from which to manage primary care.

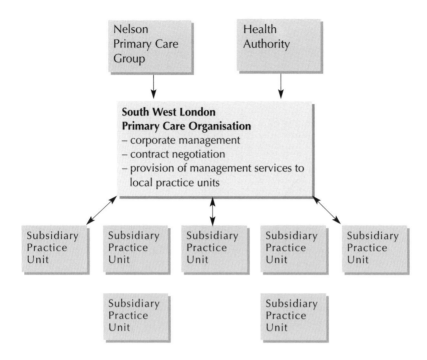

Figure 9.2: The South West London Primary Care Organisation

Overcoming fragmentation: aspirations for the future

Patients will gain access at any time to all primary, community and social care services via a single telephone number. This will include out-of-hours GP services, night nursing, intermediate care, social services, minor injuries clinics, walk-in centres and NHS Direct. All those services will have access to patient records and, in conjunction with the services provided during the day, will provide a seamless service throughout the 24-hour period. This will ensure that maximum patient care is provided in the community and will reduce the need for patients to visit A&E. Partnership working with the ambulance service and A&E ensures that patients who could be treated by the integrated care team or at a minor injuries clinic are not managed through these services. As well as the organisational integration needed there is a need for integrated IT and telecommunications equipment and co-location of the services listed above at a single centre.

Community nursing and a wide range of services currently provided by community trusts will combine with primary care services into a single team structure. Integration will work at all levels, from operational teams through service development and planning to strategic and business planning. Consideration will also be given to integrating the delivery and management of primary and community care with the social care services traditionally provided by borough-based services.

Development of a wide range of community-based diagnostic services within a polyclinic setting will enable GPs to undertake diagnostic investigations rapidly and without the need for patients to make several visits to the GP and the acute hospital.

Partnerships in a polyclinic setting with secondary care clinicians will allow the development of one-stop clinics with GP and consultant input as an alternative to the use of traditional hospital outpatient clinics. The benefits of this system would be to speed diagnosis when a consultant opinion is sought, to enable patient management to take full account of the GP's knowledge of the patient's personal circumstances, and to reduce the number of visits needed by patients. Telemedicine links could be used to supplement onsite consultant support to ensure availability of interpretative expertise throughout the day.

The PCO will build on the intermediate care services currently provided. These would cover provision of a wide range of home-based care using joint health and social service teams and workers. These services would cover the elderly, patients with chronic conditions, mental health patients and patients rehabilitating post illness or surgery. These services would be developed to optimise the management of patients in the community. A partnership will be sought with the ambulance and A&E services to ensure that appropriate use is made of intermediate care and minor injury facilities.

Conclusion

Both the Tipton and South West London PCOs are designed to meet the future needs of local people through primary care services. Many of the policy priorities of the PCO and the PCGs will be the same. Health professionals must look to their own practice, to work in partnership with others and to prioritise health inequalities. This change in culture is a radical departure from the arrangements set up in 1948.

The vehicle to deliver much of this testing agenda is primary care and the challenge for local innovators is to deliver change in attitudes, relationships and provision.

These new organisations will have an opportunity to experiment with new approaches to managing demand, including the capacity of patients to improve their self-care. PCOs can look at one of the key challenges for the NHS – the size and composition of the primary care workforce – and re-visit who does what and how. Financial and contractual issues will be important to the stability of the PCO and this affords an opportunity to look for opportunities to create incentives for continuous good practice and innovation. This is important as it sets the tone for the quality of the relationship between the health authority and the provider organisation. As integrated organisations, the PCOs can look at indicators of quality as a single organisation with multidisciplinary perspectives. One of the core tasks of the PCO is to bring together a range of primary and community provider agencies by improving the interfaces between health and social care.

PCOs will be judged by their ability to deliver improved access to, and quality of, primary care. PCOs are potentially a radical alternative, in a modernised NHS, to 50 years of centralised planning and provision of health and welfare services. The problems facing primary care will not disappear. The experimental introduction of pilot organisations such as these is a practical way of testing the appropriateness and effectiveness of national policy in a local context. Far from being last year's agenda, the PMS pilots are likely to prove to be important prototypes for new primary care organisations. The current policy framework requires PCGs to approve PMS pilots. PMS and PCGs will not be able to develop as competing alternatives. Increasingly PCGs will use PMS to pilot new ways to plan and manage the delivery of care.

References

1. Department of Health. *The New NHS – Modern, Dependable*. London: HMSO, 1997.
2. Wilkin D, Butler T and Coulter A. *New Models of Primary Care: Developing the Future*. London: King's Fund and National Primary Care Research & Development Centre, 1997.
3. Department of Health. *Primary Care: The Future*. London: HMSO, 1996.
4. Butler T. *Changing Mental Heath Services*. London: Chapman & Hall, 1993.

Chapter 10

Conclusions

Stephen Gillam and Richard Lewis

It seems strange now to recall the hullabaloo that greeted the *Choice and Opportunity* White Paper. This was the 'big bang' heralding the most radical reforms to the primary care sector since the inception of the NHS. In the event, this was not quite the case but, as Lewis and Mays point out in Chapter 2, the two White Papers that bridged the change of government had policy objectives in common, with potentially revolutionary consequences. With the first wave of PMS pilots little more than a year old, what learning can we extract for the second wave, and for fledgling PCGs? There are difficulties in attempting to generalise from the particular experiences of 80 heterogeneous sites but an early assessment of their relevance to these longstanding policy objectives is possible.

Promoting equity of service provision

PMS pilots are at least *located* predominantly in more deprived areas (see Chapter 4). Many trust-based projects are targeting particular underserved groups such as ethnic minorities, refugees or the homeless. Indications based on registration projections suggest that they are meeting previously unmet needs. However, given high staffing levels per capita, the cost effectiveness of these projects remains to be established. Will they provide a resource for other practices in their PCG? Or will they be luxuries these other practices feel they can ill afford?

Developing quality of care

For practice-based pilots, PMS has extended opportunities to develop the range and quality of services (Chapter 9). To what effect, it is too early to say. However, the NPCRDC is examining in depth the quality of care provided at 20 pilot sites using non-PMS practices as controls in a study that will examine the relative effectiveness of PMS.

While nurse-led projects have struggled to establish some of the basics of GMS, systems are in place to ensure that the quality of chronic disease management compares with the best (Chapter 5). The virtues of tighter, targeted local contracts may seem self-evident, but contracting mechanisms *per se* may have limited impact. Few first wave contracts committed their signatories to the use of specific clinical guidelines or outcome measures (Chapter 6).[1]

Encouraging responsiveness to users

Central guidance has stressed the importance of user involvement at all stages of PMS pilot development. Trust-based projects targeting priority population groups can claim with some justification to be responding to identified shortfalls. Otherwise, beyond ritualistic involvement of CHCs at the consultation stage, there is very limited evidence of user participation in the planning and development of PMS pilots.

Regarding quality of care, the early messages about patients' views are reassuring.[2] The lists of newly-established nurse-led schemes have steadily expanded. There is no evidence to suggest that pilot status has compromised the quality of medical services provided; local evaluations are starting to suggest the opposite.

Providing new flexibilities

The number of applicants to the salaried GP posts described in Chapter 6 gives an indication of their popularity. The doctors themselves have graphically described some of the advantages of salaried practice, particularly for women seeking part-time posts. These pilots have provided new opportunities for extending the role of nurses also. The 'nurse-led' pilots, in seeming to invert traditional power relations, have attracted most attention. In reality, they exhibit different degrees of 'nurse-ledness', as Jones points out. As with any other primary health care team, their success hinges less on the nature of hierarchical decision-making and more on the personal relationships that integrate team members. These are still evolving, with PMS doctors still defining how best to support nurse colleagues, and vice-versa.

These pilots represent a potentially important shift in the balance of power between the medical and nursing professions. In some respects, early nurse practitioners have been trained for a role without a context. Very often they returned with extended skills to practices unable to accommodate them. Greater independence of the sort provided by PMS pilots is long overdue.

Extending opportunities to innovate

The new Government faced a dilemma: namely how to reconcile the need for universal models that expunged the inequities of fundholding with the need to provide evolutionary opportunities for the innovative. The entrepreneurial flair of the independent general practitioner after all provides one key to the success or otherwise of primary care groups and trusts. The need to provide a safety valve for the opportunistic may explain some of their belated enthusiasm for PMS pilots.

But how innovative is innovative? These pilots seem to have been constrained by bureaucracy and regulation over such issues as nurse prescribing. Sheaff suggests that the first wave's contract documents show limited evidence of original service development (Chapter 7). PCGs are unlikely to foster diversity for its own sake. Early impressions suggest that few second wave pilots represent a coherent, strategic response to needs identified with PCGs.

What can PMS pilots contribute to evolving primary care groups?

The South West London Primary Care Organisation described in Chapter 9 – a seven practice partnership – now forms part of the Nelson Primary Care Group. The other part is a second wave PMS pilot. The whole is seeking primary care trust status in the year 2000. As Co-chairman Dr Howard Freeman says, 'We could not have got from there to here without PMS. As an intervening step it has been crucial in developing shared vision and understanding'. The barriers broken down in agreeing collectively to enter the pilot, with all the risks entailed, has led to the development of the inter-practice linkages necessary for PCTs.

Much of what the PMS initiative was designed to deliver in the way of improvements to the quality of primary care delivery is now being driven forward under the banner of clinical governance. However, the mechanisms of clinical governance alone may not be sufficiently powerful to drive forward efficient resource management in primary care. While non cash-limited GMS remained without their control, the impact of fundholders, multifunds and total purchasers on primary care provision was limited. PMS, in conjunction with primary care groups or trusts (PCTs), leads to a properly unified budget and is central in the transition to full autonomy of these new UK-style health maintenance organisatons.

PCTs may take over any existing PMS contract from the local health authority and develop their own pilots. PMS, under these circumstances, will test new corporate governance and accountability arrangements within PCTs and raises the potentially uncomfortable scenario where GPs control the very organisation that holds them to account. Accountability will be as strong or as weak as the lay-dominated board that will ultimately govern the actions of a PCT.

PMS pilots within a PCT environment also raise further issues. First, the processes of appraisal and review will be more complicated where staff are working under different conditions in practices serving different populations in different ways. Secondly, PMS provides perverse financial incentives for general practice to shift costs to the secondary sector to increase their incomes. For all its faults, the system of GMS does provide incentives for efficient behaviour. Whether PMS pilots (and therefore PCTs) are able to generate savings ('efficiency gains') within primary care without such direct incentives remains to be seen.

However, PMS pilots represent a significant new tool in the PCT toolbox. They will be able to commission primary care to address the needs of particular population groups in particular areas – local contracts with primary health care teams will help them do this, as will the option to directly salary GPs. They may need salaried posts to underpin organisational development in other ways: sessional doctors or nurses may act as substitutes for PCT board members, work out-of-hours or in 'troubleshooting' roles supporting less developed practices.

For community trusts, PMS pilots are a form of 'loss leader'. They may be costly but, as they move into partnership within PCTs, heightened understanding and capacity to manage GMS will be invaluable. They should be better placed, for example, to fuse their own clinical governance structures with those developing within PCGs.

A new millennium

The great unstated policy concern spanning the change of government, as Lewis and Mays make clear in Chapter 2, is the future of the single national contract. One of the paradoxes of the British health system is that, while GPs have always remained technically outside the NHS, they are closely identified with its strengths: 24-hour care from 'womb to tomb' for a defined list of patients. British family medicine is an object of universal admiration both for the quality of care provided and its efficiency in filtering access to specialist services. However anachronistic the notion of a family doctor, general practice is part of the nation's social fabric. Any government risks much in promoting its dissolution. The Labour Government, in developing NHS Direct, walk-in centres and other alternative points of first contact, has met with predictable professional defensiveness. But potential inefficiencies consequent upon opening up the market for primary care in this way are real. Bypassing the gatekeeper/co-ordinator risks fragmenting episodes of care, duplicating investigation and management with the generation of multiple medical records.

PMS hastens the spread of local contracting and has been seen by some to reinforce these threats. Conspiracy theorists see PMS as a key part of the plan to end general practice as we know it and replace it with a centrally planned, salaried service. This book represents an early attempt to balance pros and cons and to locate PMS within a broader context. The national programme of evaluation will yield more detailed findings.[3] Two-hundred-and-three pilots are entering the second wave. PMS remains a ripple, but one that, with gathering momentum, may yet transform primary care.

References

1. Lewis R, Gillam S, Gosden T and Sheaff R. Who contracts for primary care? *Journal of Public Health Medicine*. In press.
2. Dobson R. Patients satisfied with nurse run practices. *British Medical Journal* 1999; 319: 728.

3. Leese B, Gosden T, Riley A, Allen L, Campbell S. *Setting Out. Piloting innovations in primary care. Report on behalf of PMS National Evaluation Team.* Manchester: National Primary Care Research and Development Centre, 1999.

Appendix

The nine King's Fund and NPCRDC demonstration PMS pilot sites

Nine PMS pilot sites were selected in 1997 by the King's Fund and the National Primary Care Research and Development Centre (NPCRDC) to form a 'demonstration sites' network. The sites were chosen to reflect the mix of schemes nationally: to include both single-practice sites as well as larger groups of practices; practices with a history of working together and practices starting from scratch with a zero list; those in more affluent areas and those working in areas with high levels of deprivation; sites led by trusts, sites led by GPs and nurse-led sites.

A description of each of the nine PMS pilot sites working in collaboration with the King's Fund and the NPCRDC is given below.

Isleworth PMS pilot: The Isleworth Centre Practice

The PMS pilot in Isleworth, led by Hounslow and Spelthorne Community and Mental Health NHS Trust, employs two job-sharing GPs, a primary care nurse specialist and a wide range of primary care professionals as part of an integrated primary health care team. The pilot is based in the Isleworth Day Centre, a building previously used by the Local Authority as a day centre for the elderly and their carers, but which closed due to financial pressures.

Isleworth, with a population of 20,000 people, is located in Hounslow in west London, a borough that scores as exceptionally deprived in comparison to its surrounding suburban neighbours. Housing conditions in the area present a particular problem, and as the needs of the population have grown in the two wards of Isleworth North and Isleworth South, the level of primary care provision has fallen. In holding a contract jointly with Ealing, Hammersmith and Hounslow Health Authority, it was the Trust's aim that pilot should fill the major gap in the provision of primary care that had been identified in the area.

Patient registration at the new practice has been very rapid and, for a time, the pilot was registering 80 new patients a week. The pilot started to register patients at the beginning of September 1998, and 12 months after opening, a total of 1300 patients had joined the practice list.

North Hillingdon PMS pilot

Located in North Hillingdon, an area of average social need with pockets of deprivation, this practice-based PMS pilot serves a population of 10,000 with a high proportion of elderly people. The aim of the pilot is to bring together one group practice and two single-handed practices in order to focus on issues of demographic need, flexibility of access for patients, GP recruitment and practice administration. It will be operated in partnership with Hillingdon Health Authority.

The population in this area has high numbers of elderly and young people which '... has a significant effect on the health needs presented to our practice and a large impact on our capacity to provide and adequate level of service to our patients'. In addition, one of the single-handed practices has had problems recruiting and retaining a suitable partner to fill a vacant half-time post.

North Mersey Community Trust PMS pilot: Princess Park Health Centre

Princess Park Health Centre (PPHC) is an inner city practice consisting of six GPs and a comprehensive primary health care team, serving the deprived community in Toxteth. This pilot is also linked to the PMS pilot in Garston.

Initially, a new primary care provider directorate was established within the North Mersey Community (NHS) Trust (NMCT). This directorate then employed the existing GPs, practice staff and community nurses working at PPHC. Services are delivered, developed and managed through a PMS-plus contract between Liverpool Health Authority and NMCT.

The aim of the pilot is to unite the provision of primary care services under a single management structure, thus ensuring effective management of all primary care resources and maximising service provision. The pilot also intends to build a sustainable, flexible primary care organisation as part of a NHS Trust and provide a model that will attract and retain high quality health care professionals.

Salford nurse-led PMS pilot: The Daruzzaman Care Centre

This pilot is situated to the south of the city of Salford, forming part of the inner city. In April 1997, there were over 2000 patients being cared for by temporary locum GPs following the untimely death of a single-handed GP. This pilot was established by a nurse and is one of only two first wave nurse-led pilots where the nurse is an independent contractor. The lead nurse therefore holds the contract with the Health Authority to provide personal medical services to the population. The lead nurse also employs a salaried GP and the practice reception staff. The rest of the nursing team are employed by the local community trust.

Initially the list size for the practice was declining – as is often the case when locums cover a practice for a long period. However, once the pilot was established the list increased steadily.

The aims of the pilot are to provide a comprehensive range of services led predominantly by a nurse and create an environment where patients have direct involvement in the development and monitoring of their future health care provision.

South west London PMS pilot

The south west London PMS pilot was originally made up of eight practices with 44 GPs, working from 12 surgery premises and providing a service for 81,000 patients in the Merton, Sutton and Wandsworth Health Authority area. The practices had a history of joint working, were part of a total purchasing pilot (TPP) and although not geographically coterminous, they shared the same aims and objectives.

Whilst the area is sited in what is largely a more affluent area and does not exhibit the levels of deprivation described in other pilots, the south west London PMS pilot has identified a number of areas where they would like to see improvements made in service provision. During the first year of the pilot, a mental health facilitator has been appointed and it is planned that a pharmaceutical advisor will also be recruited to improve and co-ordinate services provided in the pilot. Other innovations planned include the increased use of intermediate care facilities with the employment of nursing care managers, improving the quality of out-of-hours services, reviewing the practice management processes and internal staffing and the introduction of personal development plans for GPs.

One of the original eight practices left the pilot in March 1999, as their practice catchment area was not coterminous with the PCG boundary of the other seven practices. The non-PMS practices making up the PCG were successful in their bid to become a second wave PMS pilot, and will now operate as a PMS site alongside the seven practices making up the first wave pilot. The Nelson PCG, within which the PMS pilot is located, is currently applying to become one of the first primary care trusts.

Streatham Hill PMS pilot: The Edith Cavell practice

The Edith Cavell practice was set up as a nurse-led pilot, co-located in existing practice premises in Streatham Hill, an area of Lambeth in south London. The skill-mix of the multidisciplinary team is significantly different from more traditional models of general practice, the intention being that patients routinely have the choice of seeing a nurse or a GP when visiting the practice for first and subsequent consultations. The nurse practitioner sees patients with undifferentiated diagnoses, and refers either to a GP or to other health professionals, as appropriate. The pilot is supported and managed by Community Health South London NHS Trust and the contract is held between the Trust and Lambeth, Southwark and Lewisham Health Authority.

The pilot places particular emphasis on the provision of personal medical services for individuals marginalised from mainstream health care, such as asylum seekers, refugees, the homeless, those with mental health problems and substance misusers – groups of people who do not readily have access to traditional models of primary care. The population to be served in the Streatham Hill area is described in the PMS pilot bid document as being 'increasingly vulnerable', with high levels of ill health and high levels of service need.

In addition to its existing list, which has grown to 1134 patients over the first 12 months of operation, the pilot will take on the patient list of the vacant practice in whose premises they are co-located, and will run this as a second wave PMS pilot.

Tipton Care Organisation

Tipton Care Organisation (TCO) is located in a deprived area in the heart of the industrial Black Country, and is bordered by the boroughs of Walsall, Wolverhampton and Dudley. Tipton has a long and sustained history of primary care development, and TCO is made up of eight practices with just under 36,000 patients. The constituent practices consist of some single-handed and some multiple doctor practices; some were previously fundholding practices. The 18 pilot GPs have formed the Tipton General Practitioner Association, which has a constitution and co-operation agreement that allows each practice to maintain its own identity and independence. The pilot holds a PMS-plus contract with the Health Authority and works very closely with the local Community Trust, Social Services departments, local patient groups and voluntary organisations.

The aims of the pilot are to provide integrated care across all agencies and communities in Tipton; to provide a greater range of services; to improve quality of, and access to, services; to provide increased efficiency and effectiveness in the utilisation of resources; and demonstrate the benefits of inter-agency working and community involvement. The 'plus' element of the contract refers to the inclusion of community nursing and allied professions and to packages of care. The care packages include both clinical and social care and cover various areas such as respiratory disease, diabetes, coronary disease prevention and orthopaedic services. The pilot also employs two salaried GPs to provide support, particularly to single-handed practices, and to further develop care management packages.

Warrington Community Healthcare NHS Trust: Appleton Primary Care

This project is a collaborative partnership between Warrington Community NHS Trust, North Cheshire Health Authority and local authorities. The project became fully operational in July 1999 and provides an innovative approach to health care delivery in a rapidly expanding area of Warrington. Residents in this new community, many of whom have moved from areas outside Warrington, have different needs from an established population.

The project was relocated to its present site after planning and construction delays hampered development in another part of the town. The pilot has a flat management structure and abolishes the role demarcations between medical and nursing clinicians. The team consists of two nurse practitioners (job-sharing), a GP and a primary care nurse (herself a graduate in nurse practitioner studies). A project manager and an informatics advisor support them. All staff are employed by Warrington Community Trust.

The pilot is a regional GP Net demonstrator site and associate site of the National Library for Primary Care. It is also an undergraduate teaching practice for Liverpool University. It is developing many aspects of clinical governance through the use of IT, without detracting from the positive experiences of primary care. Patients choose which clinician to consult and have ready access to good quality health information through the Warrington Local Evidence Centre (LMEC), which is also managed by the team.

Wolverhampton Primary Health

Wolverhampton is a multicultural urban area in the West Midlands, with diverse and challenging socio-economic characteristics. It has a population of approximately 248,000 with high levels of unemployment, deprivation, ethnic minorities and an increasing number of elderly residents. Wolverhampton has problems with the recruitment of GPs and large list sizes. Almost 50 per cent of its practices are single-handed.

A team from Wolverhampton Health Authority and Wolverhampton Healthcare NHS Trust led by Dr Tim Crossley therefore established a PMS pilot for GPs wishing to become salaried. The Trust established a directorate, 'Wolverhampton Primary Health', which exists to manage and run small practices across Wolverhampton.

The pilot manager deals with all of the day-to-day administrative tasks, co-ordinates practice staff, budgets, bulk purchasing, and holiday and sickness cover. The scheme offers GPs a team approach, which is especially helpful to single-handed GPs. GPs are attracted by incremental salaries, sick pay, study leave, maternity pay and locum cover. The lead GP, Dr Tim Crossley, also provides mentorship.

In the first wave of PMS pilots, Wolverhampton took over the management of two practices and set up one new practice in an under-doctored area. Since 1 April 1999, the NHS Executive approved a major variation to allow two more existing practices to transfer to PMS under the pilot.

A second wave application was also recently approved, which will allow the pilot to set up a further three new practices in the town. This will mean that a total of eight GPs will be employed by the Trust.

Transforming Primary Care

Personal medical services in the new NHS

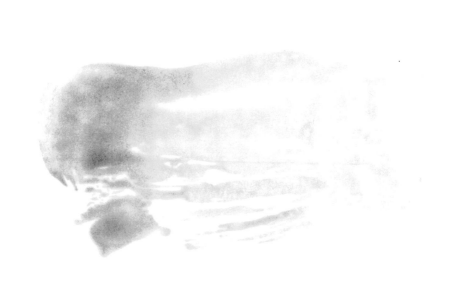